Shot in the Mouth and Still Preaching

Tom Williams

authorHOUSE°

AuthorHouse™
1663 Liberty Drive
Bloomington, IN 47403
www.authorhouse.com
Phone: 833-262-8899

Published by AuthorHouse 03/07/2023

ISBN: 979-8-8230-0301-8 (sc)
ISBN: 979-8-8230-0300-1 (e)

Library of Congress Control Number: 2023904335

Print information available on the last page.

Contents

Dedication

This book is dedicated to my hero in the faith, Terry "Shrek" Nalian. Shrek went home to be with the Lord on April 15, 2021, and I truly miss him. Shrek founded the Stand Strength Team and was an evangelist for over twenty-eight years. We have been friends for more than seventeen years, and we would challenge each other with Bible questions. This was a very special time for us, during which we grew closer to the Lord and each other. Shrek was always encouraging me to write this book, and even though I would tell him I couldn't write a book about myself, he never stopped telling me, "You should write a book about your life." One day during a phone conversation with Shrek, of which we have had many, I told him that I was stepping down as the pastor of Liberty Baptist Church. He said, "Now you have time to write the book." I don't know why, but I agreed. We came up with the title, and he told me what the first chapter should be about. I couldn't believe I was going to do it, but Shrek finally broke me down. I never dreamed that would be the last time I would talk to him, for he went home to be with the Lord about a month later at the young age of fifty-nine. It was a very hard time for me, as it was for his family and all the friends he had. I thought, *I must write this book now because that was what we talked about in our last conversation.* Well, Shrek, here it is, and the book is dedicated to you, my friend. I can't wait to see you again, but I am not writing another book.

Acknowledgments

Sandy Williams—My wife and very best friend, without whom I could have never written this book. You have been the very best encourager a person could have. I love you so much, and I thank God for giving you to me for these fifty-three years and counting. Sandy, I like you a lot!

Jen Vaughn—For all the time you put into my book when you did all the initial proofreading. You had a lot of patience and were very kind in showing me all my errors, and I do mean *all*. Thank you, Jen!

Luke Vaughn and Rick Allerton—For not just helping me with the computer stuff but *doing* most of it. Computer is a foreign language to me, and I would still be working on it were it not for your help. Thanks, guys!

Santino Vitale—For designing the front cover of the book. Who would have thought that, after knowing you when you were just hours old, you would be making me look good on the front cover of this book? Santino, thank you!

Anastasia Miller—For doing all the work on the photos and making them presentable for the book, which I know was some work for you, and for allowing me to come to your work to bug you about the photos. Anastasia, thank you!

In Vietnam

About six months earlier, I graduated from Perry High School in Massillon, Ohio. Then I found myself in Vietnam on a troop carrier going back to where soldiers had been killed and wounded. They needed replacements, and I was one of them. When I first flew into Vietnam, I thought for sure I would get shot when I was getting off the plane, but nothing happened and we stepped on Vietnamese ground without any gunfire. The next day, the leaders lined all of us rookies up and told us that we were now infantrymen. We were replacing one third of the Forty-Seventh Infantry Regiment, Ninth Infantry Division.

I had gone through basic training at Fort Knox, Kentucky, where I was trained as a tank driver, so naturally I was ready to receive my keys for the tank I would be driving. The soldier beside me was trained as a clerk and was looking for his typewriter—but things do change in times of war. I thought, *Okay, so I won't be driving a tank. That's not so bad. How much worse could it be?* I knew I wasn't supposed to think things like that. But I was in for one more surprise—they said I would be carrying the radio. I had no idea how much a radio weighed, but someone told me it was about fifty pounds. Remember, I had just graduated from high school six months earlier and was only seventeen years old. I figured that would be it for the surprising news, but it wasn't. They told me I would be walking point, which meant I would be about one hundred yards in front of the rest of the guys.

So in a few short days, I went from driving a tank on dry ground to walking in rice paddies and crossing rivers in front of the other guys. I didn't realize how dangerous this job was or that the chance of survival was very small—and I do mean *very small*. Many years later, I watched a documentary that revealed that infantrymen carrying radios and walking point got shot every fifty-four seconds. I'm really glad I didn't know this at the time. The enemy wanted to cut off all communications, so when they saw an antenna waving around in the air, that was the first thing they shot at. And by walking in front of the other guys—well, you get the picture. I said my new job was to be a human guinea pig because we were to spot the enemy first. If they spotted us first, they would shoot at us first.

So there I was, weighing in at a whopping 138 pounds and carrying a radio on my back weighing about 50 pounds. I also carried a .45-caliber pistol, an M-16 rifle, many hand grenades, a lot of M-16 clips, smoke grenades, and other stuff—altogether weighing about 70 pounds. If you double that weight, it would come to 140 pounds, so I was carrying half my body weight every time we went in the field. I never did know why they didn't give the radio to someone who weighed about 200 pounds.

It was only about six years earlier that I had played with toy soldiers in my safe backyard. And two years earlier, I got my driver's license. My life had truly taken sharp turn in a few short years. But I did volunteer for the military, so this isn't a complaint—just letting you know where I was at that time. I will admit that I didn't like the thought of walking on very wet terrain instead of driving a big tank on dry ground, but somehow I understood why I got the assignment. These soldiers must have been through a lot and needed help, so why shouldn't we go and help them out?

When I first put that radio on my back, I thought I was going to tip over backward. It truly was heavy, and I thought, *How in the world am I going to do this?*

Okay, let's get back to the troop carrier. I couldn't believe we'd be working with the navy. My dad had been in the navy, so I thought this was really neat. We were going to someplace where a lot of soldiers had been either killed or wounded, and they needed help. We loaded up the carrier, and I was the last one on, which meant I would be the first one off. When that thought came to my mind, being the first one off, I thought of the war movies I had seen. The first soldiers who got off these carriers would be shot as soon as they ran off. Listen, I was no John Wayne, storming up the beach. I was a 138-pound guy carrying 70 pounds of equipment. I was thinking, *How am I going to be able to move, let alone run?*

I really thought I was going to throw up; in fact, I'm not sure I didn't. I think I swallowed it because I didn't want the other soldiers thinking I was some kind of wimp. I knew I was not the only one going through this experience. Someone yelled out, "Here we go! Get ready!" I really thought I was going to die as soon as the doors came crashing down. It had taken about two hours to get to where we were going, but it seemed like two days.

You have heard the saying, "My whole life flashed before me." Well, let me tell you—it's true. My whole life flashed before my eyes, from playing with my two sisters in our backyard to going into high school; my first date with my now wife, Sandy; and on and on. When I had sat on my backyard swing thinking, *What am I going to do when I graduate from high school?* this moment that was about to happen had not even been on my list. I was only eighteen, going on thirty. I was thinking, *What's going to happen to me when that door drops down?* I can't even discribe all the emotions I was going through at the time, but there were plenty of them. This was just the start of all the new emotions I was going to have in the next year. The doors started to open, and I got my first glimpse of the shores of Vietnam. Before I tell you what happens next, let me go back to how my life started.

Growing Up

I was born July 18, 1949. As I'm writing this book, I am seventy-two years old, which is hard for me to believe. My parents are Jack and Jean Williams, and I have two sisters, Pat and Jackie. I didn't realize it at the time, but I had a great childhood, which my grandkids love to hear me talk about. Some of you reading this right now might be shaking your head in agreement and wondering where the years went; they were much simpler days indeed. Our first home was on the southwest side of Canton, Ohio, and was heated by coal, which later was converted to natural gas. I know—it was high class.

At about five years old, I would walk down to the local mom-and-pop store about five blocks away from our house. Listen to this: I would walk by myself to the store with one nickel in my pocket and buy five pieces of candy. It would take a while to get these five pieces of candy because there were two or three shelves of penny candy, and it was hard to choose. My parents didn't even think of something happening to me because nothing happened to children walking the streets back then. It was truly safe, and parents didn't have to think, *Will my child get kidnapped?* We had "guards" called moms and dads watching us from all the houses surrounding us. We knew our neighbors, and my parents knew they would be on guard. If something went wrong, they were there to help—and I mean something wrong like falling out of a tree, getting hit by a baseball, or even getting hit by a car because you were not watching where you were going.

Accidents like that could have happened back then, but they did not happen to me. When my kids were growing up, the environment had changed, and not for the good. I would not let my five-year-old child walk the streets alone to anyplace. I didn't know my neighbors because everyone was so busy, and the homes were not like before. The word *trust* came up a lot because so much bad stuff was happening to kids, and parents had to be very careful about where their kids went. So the backyard was the only place they could go by themselves. What a shame.

My mom and dad moved us to a small town called Richville, Ohio, and it was the same way there. I often went to a park about five blocks away from our house to play sports with the local kids. I would ride my bike to Richville Park, about three miles away, to play baseball about every other day. I was about ten years old at the time. I know it sounds crazy, but that was life then. Again, all of us kids had many moms and dads watching us just as well as my own mom and dad would.

Another park that was across the street from us was called Timken Park, and it was our Disney World. Let me tell you how blessed I was to live right across the street from it. It had a big fishing lake, four tennis courts, three horseshoe pits, two shuffleboard courts, and a huge basketball court that was filled with water in the winter so we could ice skate. It also had four baseball fields and a huge playground with sprinklers we could run through. It was a paradise in Richville. I never realized how great I had it until I started having kids myself.

I would spend almost the whole day there, and when my mom wanted me to go back home, she would hang a bedsheet from the upstairs window. As soon as I saw the sheet, I would head home. It was our little system, and it worked really well. Now, it was a different story with my dad. When he wanted me, he would just yell out my name, and he only had to yell it out once. If he had to yell it twice, the end result would not be good for me. My dad was an old-school dad; he expected us to listen and behave, which is a foreign thing today. If we got in trouble at school, we would get a paddling from the teacher or principal and another one when we got home. It was so different back then—parents stayed married to each other for life, kids were safe to go anywhere without any fear of something happening to them, the doors to people's homes were never locked unless they were on vacation, neighbors were really neighbors, and people could trust one another. I even took my shotgun to school with me, leaving it in the car, because I would go hunting right after school, and I never locked my car.

I do not know what happened to those days, but everything has changed for families today. Having one mom and one dad in a home is a rarity today, and children need it because it provides structure. Today, police officers walk up and down the halls of schools because some disgruntled kid may come into any school and start shooting other kids without even knowing them. I don't let my wife go to the mall at night by herself and sometimes even during the day. During my childhood, even people who got bullied didn't think of shooting that person, let alone anybody else. I got bullied at times in school and never thought of anything like that, but today is a different story. Our kids do not know what it was like during my childhood; in fact, it sounds too good to be true. But it was so good to live back then. Listen, I would leave the house in the morning and come back at suppertime, and my parents would not ask me where I had been all day. They knew I was safe. For Christmas or my birthday, I would get air guns, BB guns, and pellet guns, and of course, I would get an intense safety course from my dad. He said, "Don't point the gun at another human being." I looked at him, puzzled, and said, "Why would I do that? I won't." I passed the safety test and went into the woods looking for something to shoot, or I put up some of my old toys and shot them. That was good, wholesome fun for a twelve-year-old kid, and it took up the day.

I never dreamed in a million years that, just six years later I would be on a troop carrier in Vietnam ready to be dropped off in a place where I thought I had a good chance of dying. Six years earlier, I was shooting plastic ships in my backyard or dividing my toy soldiers into the good guys and bad guys. I can remember my dad taking me on my first hunt to look for rabbits. My dad would say, "When you see the rabbit run, aim your gun just ahead of him and shoot." But then, I was suddenly eighteen years old and carrying a Colt 45 pistol, an M-16 rifle, and many hand grenades. My boot camp sergeant told me, "When you see the guy running with his rifle, start shooting at him." It is no wonder my mom cried for months when I volunteered for the army; she knew all these things that were about to happen to me, and I was her baby boy. We had already lost someone from our neighborhood in Vietnam, so that was on my mom's mind and I sure my dad's too. I did not think about dying too much. I just wanted to get my two years in and get back home to start my life.

Back on the Carrier

I felt the carrier hit the ground. My heart was beating around 150 times a minute, and I am not going to lie—I was shaking like a leaf. Once we were on the ground, the carrier crew did not waste any time dropping the door, and there it was, the place where many of our soldiers had been killed or wounded. The navy had done their job, and they must have been thinking, *Come on, you army guys. Get off the carrier so we can get going.* And I don't blame them. As I looked out, all I could see were trees, so I ran off the carrier with a heart rate of two hundred beats a minute and saying to myself, *What am I doing here? I am going to die within my first few steps.* I immediately started to look for a big rock or tree stump to hide behind. I didn't even notice that no bullets were being fired at us. It's funny—and I don't mean "ha ha" funny—how things went in slow motion. It seemed like it took me a very long time to get to the big rock I hid behind, but I know that, being really scared like I was and running very fast with all the weight I was carrying, it was only a few seconds. After I settled behind the big rock and started to feel a little safe, our company commander yelled, "Come on, you guys! Get up and keep moving forward!"

Let me interject something here: during my stay in Vietnam, I would often say things to myself that came from my civilian training, and this was one of those times. Quietly, I said, "Are you crazy? Why leave a perfectly safe place like this big rock?" I knew he would not listen to my reasoning, so I called on my army training, got up, and started to advance. We walked into the wooded area and started to see evidence that a lot of things had happened there. All kinds of debris was strewn everywhere,

8

like M-16 cartridges, tree limbs, and—for the first time in my life—body parts. I almost got sick to my stomach again, but this time it was because of what I was seeing, not what I was about to do. Either way I was sick to my stomach. Another saying came to mind at this time: I wasn't in Kansas anymore, meaning I was not playing with toy soldiers in my backyard. This was the real thing. I truly believe that, at that very moment, I matured ten years and realized I had better *stay* in army-training mode from then on. I was not watching a John Wayne war movie; this was the real deal, and I was in the middle of it. It was still hard for me to believe that, about six months earlier, I had walked across the stage to receive my high school diploma.

Our company commander got us all together and planned the rest of the day for us. He started out by addressing me and two other guys; I can't remember their names. He said, "You guys will walk ahead of us to spot the VC (Viet Cong) before we get there." At first, I thought we must be special since we were chosen to do this very special mission, but after a while I realized that we were just soldiers doing our jobs. Nothing to see here. I still did not know that the soldier carrying the radio was the number-one target of the VC, and I am glad I did not know. I would have been so scared, thinking that I was going to get shot at any moment. The death rate of soldiers carrying the radio and walking point was around 95 percent. It is because that stupid long antenna waves in the air saying, *Here I am! Shoot me!* But again, I didn't know this. I thought I was special because I called in air strikes and always knew what was going on because, most of the time, it went through me. But hey, I was just picked for my good looks.

So began my first day as a radio-carrying soldier with a fifty-pound radio on my back, only eighteen years old. I look at eighteen-year-old kids today and say to myself, *Wow. Was I that young in the jungles of Vietnam?* Most of us had been given nicknames, and some of them were obvious, like Slim, Lefty, and Tex. Mine was Kid because I was just a kid. I was the youngest soldier in my company. At first, I didn't like it, but it started to grow on me, and eventually I wrote on my helmet "The Kid." As I was walking point with these two other guys, we walked through brush, woods, rice paddies, and small creeks. Remember, this was the same place where many soldiers had died and been wounded, so I was waiting for something to happen, like the VC to run out and start shooting at us or one of us stepping on a booby trap. We walked all day, and nothing happened. I was very thankful for that, but I knew it was only a matter of time. It was like being a fireman trained to put out fires, but during your shift, no fire calls came in. You're glad that you didn't have any fire calls because you didn't have to experience the sadness of someone being hurt or killed in the fire. This is how I felt every time we went out and didn't get into a firefight. We were trained to kill the enemy or be killed, but since we saw no enemy that day, we could count it as one day when we didn't have to kill anyone or watch anyone in our own outfit get killed or wounded. We had been trained to deal with both situations. I am so glad I received the training I got because, at times, it did save my life.

Training at Fort Knox, Kentucky

As I have said, I was seventeen years old when I graduated from high school. During this time, almost every guy who graduated from high school was drafted when they turned nineteen, unless they had medical problems. I have no idea where it came from, but at some point I thought, *I don't want to wait until I'm nineteen years old and then get drafted*—because I knew I would be drafted at that time. I wanted to get it over with, so I heard that people could volunteer for the military and serve their two years immediately. The only thing was that, at my age, I had to get my parents to sign a permission slip. I had no idea how it was going to turn out, but I did get enough nerve to ask them. My dad was a little disappointed because he had been in the navy along with all his brothers, so I was the first to go into another branch of service. On the other hand, he was also very proud of me for making this mature decision at such a young age, so he signed the permission slip. Even to this day, I really do not know where that decision came from, but I do know this: What happened in Vietnam changed so much of my thinking on so many things. Honestly, even though I said I don't know where that thought came from, I really do, and I will explain it later.

Next, I had to get my mom to sign the permission slip, which is another story. She asked me one simple but very important question: "Why do you want to do this?" I really could not give her an answer that was going to satisfy her. I was a mama's boy and her favorite child—a fact that even my two sisters reluctantly accepted. Now listen, I know parents are not supposed to have favorites, and I know that my mom truly loved my two sisters like no other mom could, but there was something about Mom and me that I can't explain. Even today my sister will say, "Mom loved you more than us," and of course I have to agree with her, with a sheepish grin on my face. My mom really did not want to do let me join the military, but with tears running down her face and staining the permission slip, she signed it. I felt bad for making her cry so much, but it helped to see the proud look on my dad's face. So it was done. It was settled—when I graduated from school, I would enter the United States Army in a few short weeks. During those months before I graduated, I really didn't think about it much. But when my time to report was only days away, racing through my mind was the thought, *What have I done?* I kept thinking about how much my mom cried and how much I would miss my girlfriend Sandy. Two years started to sound like a long time.

This is a photo of my two favorite women in the world: Sandy, my wife, and my mom.

A lot of my friends in school thought I was nuts for enlisting. We already knew of people from our school who had been killed or wounded in Vietnam. But I kept thinking, *When my two years are over, I will only be nineteen years old.* That is what I kept telling them and myself, even though two years did seem like a very long time. I graduated from high school, and about a month later I went into the army about as green as a person can get and without knowing a single person. I must admit that, at times during my first trip, I thought, *What in the world have I done? Maybe I am crazy.* My school buddies were back home, still celebrating graduation from high school, and here I was heading off to boot camp in the hottest time of the year at Fort Knox, Kentucky. I didn't know what was ahead of me, so I figured I must be crazy. I believe the jury is still out on that.

When the time came, I boarded a train to head for my first station. The train finally arrived at Fort Knox, and as soon as I deboarded, I heard some guy yelling, "Get over here and stand on this line!" I joined the many other guys who were already standing on the line. It was amazing to me that guys from all over the United States were standing on this line—from New York to California—and all of us had the same look on our faces. I cannot even describe that look, but we all saw it. It might be called a scared look or a *What have I done?* look, or maybe an *I was just kidding—I want to go back home* look, but it was a look.

What happened next would change all of our lives for the next two months. The drill sergeant came out to greet us—and I don't mean in a *Welcome, guys, I hope you enjoy your stay with us* way. This drill sergeant was about nine feet tall and weighed about five hundred pounds. You might think I'm exaggerating, but you were not there to witness this giant of a man. Before I go on, let me say something about being raised by my dad. He was a no-nonsense, strict dad, as most were back in those days. If dads were graded on strictness, my dad would have received an A plus with extra bonus points. My dad loved us and always took care of us, and we never lacked for anything; but he wanted us to do two main things: be good and listen to him no matter what. This is what we need in homes today; we have so many unruly kids who do not have the structure that I had. I did think at times that my dad was unfair, making me be good and listen to him—and I am saying this sarcastically. So there I was, standing on the line thinking about how I had enlisted in an effort to get away from my dad and his always telling me what to do and that maybe I would be able to make some of my own decisions. You may be wondering, *Did you really think that is how boot camp was going to be?* And my answer at that time would have been yes. All I know is that my dad had nothing on this drill sergeant, and I do mean nothing. He did not give a nice, welcoming speech. In fact, he opened with this: "From now on, boys, I will be your mama and your daddy, and you will do one thing and one thing only—listen to me and nobody else for the next two months. I will tell you when you can sleep, when you get up, when you eat, when you walk, and even when you can breathe." The first thoughts that came to mind were, *What have I done?* and *Could this man be stricter than my dad?* I know now that was a foolish thought because my dad was a Boy Scout compared to this drill sergeant, whom I had only known for about five minutes. There were about thirty of us guys standing on that line, and I do believe I saw some tears falling from some of their faces. But this New York street kid chuckled a little after hearing our first instructions. The next thing that happened changed my thinking on how I was going to handle my next two months. The drill sergeant heard this guy chuckle and immediately ran over to him. I do believe his nose was touching the guy's nose, and he started to yell, "Do you have a problem with that? And if you do, the next thing that you will remember is picking yourself off the ground and

14

we will repeat this until you do understand it!" I really do not know what happened, but the New York street kid was soon picking himself up off the ground and bleeding from the nose. You might be thinking, *How could he do that? He should be fired.* But please, listen to me—he was getting us ready for war, and I do mean *war,* in which we would have to fight for our lives and those of the guys next to us. This was not a Boy Scout troop; this was the army, and this drill sergeant was going to try to make us soldiers ready for battle. One of the things my dad told me before I left was, "Do what they say, and don't have an attitude about it. Rolling your eyes will get you in serious trouble." That advice was accurate; I saw it in the very first minutes of being in boot camp. Well, this drill sergeant definitely got our attention right away, which was his plan. He was telling and showing us that he meant business.

We all started to walk toward this big building with our street clothes and different haircuts, which identified who we were and even what part of the country we had come from. In just a few short hours, though, we were walking out of that building wearing green army-issue fatigues and heavy black boots, and we all had the same haircut, which was very short. That way, we all started on the same level, and most of us couldn't remember what we had looked like when we entered that building.

The next day, it all started. We got up very early, and the first thing we did was run. Then we ate breakfast, but it was not a sit-down-and-relax meal; it was a timed meal, and the allotted time was only a few minutes. My wife has always said that I eat too fast—well, this is why. I was trained to eat fast, and that training has never left. So blame it on that big old mean drill sergeant. At one point—and I'm not sure why I thought this—I told myself that I was going to do the very best I could, no matter what everybody else did. I believed that this drill sergeant was going to train us to be good soldiers and that his training might save our lives, even though his methods were like nothing I have ever seen. Maybe I thought this because I already knew that some of my friends had been killed or wounded in Vietnam, that this was a real thing that was happening, and that I would be in Vietnam very soon. I look back on this boot camp training and think two months was not a very long time to train someone to be a soldier going off to war. To be a good doctor, people go through at least eight years of training, and to be a good lawyer, they go through at least four years of training. So training people to be good soldiers seemed like it should take more than two months of boot camp and two months of advanced training. Regardless, I graduated from boot camp and was glad it was over. Later, I found out that the drill sergeant was a really nice guy; of course, I couldn't have known this until the training was over. I turned eighteen while in boot camp and didn't even get a birthday party. Imagine that.

This is a photo of Sandy and me after boot camp training, in 1967, some sixty days after graduating from high school.

The next training was advanced individual training (AIT) and was also done at Fort Knox. This was another two months of training but without the intense yelling and screaming. I would be training to be a tank driver, which I thought was pretty cool, but I didn't know then that I would not even see a tank in Vietnam because the terrain was too wet. My attitude did not change in AIT: I wanted to truly learn and be the very best tank driver. Think about this—the first car I owned was a 1947 Ford with "suicide doors," four doors that opened away from one another. Some of my friends called it a tank because it was so big. And then, there I was, eighteen years old and just a few years after learning how to drive a car, suddenly learning how to drive a tank, an honest-to-goodness army tank. It was very cool, I must admit. After two months of AIT training, we received our orders—everyone was going to Vietnam except for three of us who had orders to Germany. I had mixed emotions about this. On one hand, I was mad because I wanted to go to Vietnam; on the other hand, I thought, *I am not going to Vietnam, and in Germany they will not be shooting at me.* But about three days later, our orders changed. We were in fact going to Vietnam, and once again I had mixed emotions. But the emotions my mom experienced were extreme. She cried for quite a while once my orders were changed. At this point, I was not afraid even though I had some good friends who had been killed or wounded there. My brother-in-law was badly wounded in Vietnam, but of course I thought it would not happen to me. But the moment the plane doors open after landing in Vietnam, my thinking changed. Below is a photo of Sandy and me before I left for Vietnam. I left as an eighteen-year-old kid but came back as a combat-wounded Vietnam War soldier.

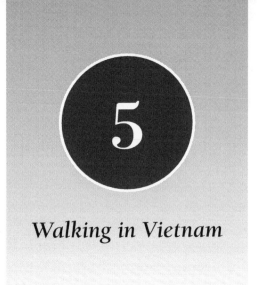

Walking in Vietnam

I quickly understood why my training at Fort Knox included a lot of running—and I do mean *a lot*. The big test was when we ran up a hill called Agony Hill wearing all our gear and heavy army boots. The definition of *agony* is extreme physical or mental suffering, and that is the best description of Agony Hill. It was brutal, but once in Vietnam, I saw why it was so necessary. It built up our leg muscles, which really had to be strong while we were in Vietnam. Walking was the main thing infantrymen did there, in all kinds of conditions. The below photo shows me after walking through some deep water—which was always fun—while carrying about seventy pounds of stuff on my back, around my waist, across my shoulders, and even on my head. It is hard to believe that I was able to do that.

I look back now and want to thank the drill sergeant for pushing us so hard because, without that training, it would have been impossible to make it through all the conditions we walked in.

We would get leeches while walking in the creeks and rivers that we had to cross. I understood why they were called bloodsuckers—because that is exactly what they did. Some guys cried when they took off their clothes after crossing the creeks and rivers because they were covered with leeches, and I do mean *covered*. In some places, we couldn't walk across because the water was too high, and in others, we would start to cross and then find ourselves literally in over our heads. That was one of my fears. I was carrying about seventy pounds of stuff, and it truly is hard to swim with all that weight. We didn't receive that type of training at Fort Knox, but I could see why: most likely, it's a situation that would not come up.

In those cases, we had to use whatever we could to cross the water or walk farther to find a safe crossing. Traveling by canoe was quite an experience. Piling all the soldiers into one canoe with all that weight made for a real amusement park ride—without the addmission fee or amusement. It was a real trip and, I will tell you, very scary. The definition of *scary* is frightening and causing fear, which it did. Maybe amusement parks could design a ride after this experience. But I would not ride it; it's too frightening.

After walking around for miles and miles without running into any VC, we would go on to our next place—and that meant flying in a helocopter. I was only eighteen years old, so this was a fun time for me. I didn't realize it at the time, but it took my mind off where I was. I would actually sit with my feet hanging over the edge, looking at all the scenery, and the helicopter would fly as close as it could to the trees because it was harder for the VC to see them coming that way. Although these were quite the ride, I didn't like where they were taking us—another place to try and find the VC.

The pilot and others in the helicopter had very dangerous jobs, as they were always out in the open and exposing themselves to gunfire. I truly looked up to them for what they were doing and how they always were looking out for us. They flew soldiers to place after place every day, and I was amazed at how brave they were. Helicopter gunner was one of the most dangerous jobs in Vietnam. We lost many brave soldiers doing it, so if you were a gunner in Vietnam, I salute you and say, "Welcome home. You made it."

The helicopter ride was my mental escape from where I was and where I was going next. Every time I hear a helicopter, even today, it takes me back to Vietnam.

When we walked, we would usually come to a small village and ask the people there if they had seen any VC. Most of the time they would say no because they truly feared the VC. The villagers were generally innocent people trying to live peaceful lives for themselves and their children. The war had been going on for many years, and they were just as tired of it as we were. They had seen many of their children be killed or badly wounded in the conflict. The VC would walk into their villages and ask them if they had seen any American GIs, but if they said no, the VC, being very ruthless people, would beat them badly or kill them, including children, and sometimes they would burn down their homes.

This is one of the reasons they were so tired of the war going on in their backyards and being bombed all the time. I couldn't even imagine this going on in my neighborhood for years and years. Depending on to whom they said no, they could suffer physical harm or death. What a way to live. I have never had any nightmares about Vietnam, for which I am so thankful, but I do have one memory that still comes to my mind at times—the orphanages full of kids who lost their parents because of this war.

I loved interacting with the children. This photo shows me clowning around with one of them.

The American military lost many soldiers in Vietnam, and many of them had children, which is a tradegy for so many who will never get over it. I have seen burnt bodies of children after a village bombing, which I will never forget. I realize that this will happen during a war, but when you actually see it with your own eyes, smell the burnt flesh, see dead bodies everywhere, and hear the people crying over the deaths of their children, it stays with you. We lost 58,220 soldiers during the Vietnam War and many more were wounded, so it is hard for me to even talk about this part of war. Vietnam was over fifty years ago, and there are still many people who are affected by it.

Going back to my first week there, when we walked around looking for the VC unsuccessfully, it was a good way to ease into what we were going to be doing all the time. It gave us all a chance to get a little more used to walking with all the weight we were carrying over the terrain. After the first week in the field or in the bush, we went back to our base camp, which was called Bearcat. We spent two or three day there healing from the mosquito bites, red ant bites, leech bites, and ringworm. The two main priorities were resting up and catching up on our mail. Oh, baby! Did someone say "mail call"?

Mail Call

Mail call then was so different from mail call today. The soldiers today have cell phones, so they can talk to just about anyone at anytime from anywhere. Soldiers overseas can watch their babies being born, weddings, and their children's graduations. Now, don't get me wrong: I would have loved to have a cell phone in Vietnam instead of mail call, especially considering that today's cell phones are not just devices for talking to people. You can watch movies and sporting events and play almost any game you want. How great would that have been in Vietnam? I can remember watching movie detective Dick Tracy talking on his wristwatch and thinking, *Yeah, like that would ever happen*. But today my wife has a phone on her wrist, and she is not Dick Tracy.

Anyway, in 1967and 1968 in Vietnam, mail call time was the highlight of most soldiers' days. When we heard "mail call" being yelled out, we dropped everything—and I do mean everything. It would be like a man coming to the end of your street and yelling out, "It's money time!" He would call the name of a person who lived on that street, and that person would win one million dollars. You would be waiting for the man to yell it out each time and run in hopes of hearing your name called out, most likely shaking with anticipation, because one million dollars would change your life. When you didn't hear your name, you would be so disappointed, but you could hardly wait for the next time. Well, that is exactly what mail call was like in Vietnam, and that is no exaggeration. When I didn't hear my name called out during mail call, it felt like that nine-foot-tall drill sergeant had punched me in the gut—it knocked the wind out of me. I would actually get jealous of the soldiers who did get mail, and if someone receive more than one piece of mail, that felt unfair and made me wonder why everyone back in the States hated me. That sounds a little strong, I know, but I am telling you—mail call was the most important thing that happened in Vietnam, except for flying home. But, oh buddy, when I *did* hear my name called, "Williams, Thomas," I started to walk down the red carpet to receive my Oscar award, and everyone around was smiling and hoping their names would be called next. The guys would always make way for me to get my one million dollars—whoops, I mean letter, same thing. You may be thinking that comparing a letter to one million dollars or an Oscar award is exaggerating, but I beg you to believe me when I say how important mail call was because it truly was. There are no words strong enough to convey that it was the heartbeat of the soldiers in Vietnam.

When I wrote letters to my mom, Sandy, my sisters, and friends, they would take a week or more to get to them. It took that same amount of time for their letters to reach me after they mailed them. Think about that in comparison to the fast-paced world in which we live today. A few months ago, I received a call from a missionary friend of mine from Africa, and we talked for about half an hour. When I hung up the phone, I told the people who were with me, "I just talked to someone from Africa. Can you believe that he picked up his cell phone and pushed a button, and immediately my phone rang?" In Vietnam, It took two weeks or more to get answers to any questions that I asked my mom. Two weeks! When I finally received a letter with her answer, sometimes I had forgotten what my question was.

Mail call was not always a happy time, though, because sometimes a name would be called out and everyone would realize that soldier had been killed. Everyone would go silent, and sometimes we cried, which I almost did while writing this down. Those letters were not supposed to make it to mail call, but accidents happen when there is so much going on. Also, some soldiers got "Dear John" letters, meaning that their wives, fiancées, or girlfriends were leaving them. This was a great time of sorrow for those soldiers, made more difficult because they couldn't talk to the senders right away. It took two weeks or more to receive answers to their letters asking why.

I loved getting letters from my mom, dad, sisters, and friends, but when I received a letter from Sandy, it was like, *Look out, heart! Here come about four hundred more beats a minute.* I walked differently and smiled longer after I got one of her letters. I would read each letter over and over, and it would go out to the bush with me so I could read it some more. Many soldiers would put those types of letters in their helmets so they would be easy to get to. As a side note, the Sandy who wrote those letters has been my wife for over fifty-two years now. They were God sent; it seemed like they always came at the right time, when I was down and really missing home. I truly felt bad for the soldiers who never received any letters, and I mean never. They would not even come to mail call because they knew their names would not be called. This was truly sad. This is why, when I came home, I told people who knew someone in Vietnam to send them letters or a store advertisement or *something.* I cannot emphasize enough how important it was to hear my name being called out during mail call. "Williams, Thomas"—I just won a million dollars!

Receiving a box from home sent an extra shot of adrenaline through my body. I received the box of the year—maybe of the whole Vietnam era— from my sister, Pat. Getting a box created a different type of excitement because a box could hold anything, while letters were words on a page. A box could have something to eat, to read, or to wear, like boxer shorts with hearts all over them, which I will explain later on. When I got the box from my sister, I slowly opened it and first saw popcorn. I love popcorn, so this was a great gift. I started to think, *Wait a minute. The box is really heavy, so what else is in it?* I started to remove the popcorn, meaning I ate it, and finally saw what was in the box. I could not believe it! How did she manage to send me a watermelon? Yes! I said *a watermelon.* She had sent it when it was a little green, so by the time it arrived it was ripe. What I am about to tell you may not seem very nice and a little stingy, but I ate that whole watermelon, along with all the popcorn, all by myself. Have you ever seen a bunch of piranhas attack a piece of meat? Well, that would have been my watermelon if the guys had known I had it. How could I share a six-inch watermelon with thirty guys? So what I did was for their own good. That is my story, and I am sticking to it. I did have to eat it fast because the smell of watermelon goes through the air quickly. After I finished it, I did something that I am not proud of—I let the watermelon rinds sit out so the guys could smell it, and of course even that stirred the piranhas up. They went into a frenzy. I have been talking about that watermelon for years, and I am sure the guys who were there are still talking about it too. So Pat, once again, thank you!

Besides getting mail and eating popcorn and watermelon, we would play football anytime we could. For some reason, the photo below is one of my favorites from Vietnam. When I show this to people, most of them think that we were running from the enemy or toward a bunker to get away from a mortar attack. In reality, it is a bunch of guys getting relief from the war by playing football. If you look closely, you can see the football in the air. It is on the left side above the first group of guys.

The games could get rough at times—I believe because they were a good way to relieve our frustrations of being in a war. It was always like the helicopter ride for me: it put my mind in a different spot. At these football games, we were playing in the Super Bowl game every time and trying to make a touchdown to win the game instead of shooting at someone or watching someone die or get wounded or picking off leeches from our bodies. It was very good for every soldier to have a release like this, whether football or playing cards. We had to have an escape. Sometimes we would sit around and talk about the last time we had been out in the bush, which was also a good way to release our emotions to one another. It is hard for men to share what they are really thinking, and sometimes we are truly thinking nothing. But when we would sit around and start talking, I must admit it got pretty emotional at times, but it was a good thing for us. We were soldiers trained to kill our enemies, and our thinking was that real soldiers don't cry. I was eighteen years old, and I was shooting at people and trying to kill them. This is very heavy stuff for a young mind to digest. When I saw one of my good friends get shot and killed or badly wounded, that was more heavy stuff for my mind to digest. I know I have said it before, but it bears repeating: just about six years earlier, I was playing with my two-inch plastic soldiers in my safe backyard, and then I was in a war.

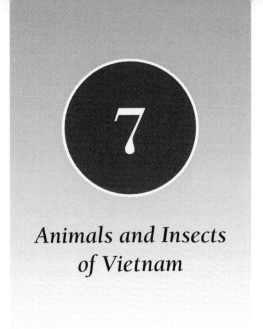

7

Animals and Insects of Vietnam

Even though Vietnam is home to about two hundred types of snakes, for some strange reason I did not see even one snake, which is truly strange and a blessing. I walked for miles and miles in rice paddies, swamps, creeks, rivers, and the bush, and it would make sense that I would have seen at least one snake. I am not afraid of snakes; I like them and think they are cool. It was a blessing that I did not see any because I know myself, and I would have tried to pick them up or play with them. Picking up a snake in Vietnam is not a good thing to do because many of them are venomous.

I did see rats, though, and they were as big as some dogs back home. The first description I heard of a rat was from a group of kids when we were walking around their village. They said they were going to get "number one chop chop," which meant they were going rat hunting for a meal. They would gather around a tree, and one kid would shimmy up to the top of the tree and begin to shake it by swaying back and forth. The other kids would be waiting at the bottom of the tree with rocks in their hands, ready to beat the rat until it died. They would do this until they got enough rats for everyone and then go home, and their mom would cook the rats for their meal. If you think that is disgusting, you must know that there was no garbage in these villages because the people never threw away food, so for them eating a rat was like eating a rabbit or cow for us. The rats were very clean animals; they were a lot cleaner than the chickens in the States, and I know that because I raised chickens at one time. They eat anything, and I do mean anything. I never tried eating rat meat, but I would have if I had gotten the chance.

Another plentiful animal was the water buffalo, which was a gigantic animal. Each one weighed anywhere from fifteen hundred to twenty-six hundred pounds and was about nine feet long from head to tail, and then the tail alone was about three feet long. It stood about four feet tall, so, like I said, it was a gigantic animal. Farmers used them like tractors. They did everything from plowing to removing rocks and whatever else was needed. I don't know why, but water buffalo did not like American soldiers very much; we had to watch them carefully when we passed by them because they would come after us. One day we stopped to rest after walking through a rice paddy for a few hours. When I wasn't walking point, which I was most of the time, I walked with the lieutenant so he could talk on the radio. We were sitting on a patch of dry land next to the rice paddy, and a water buffalo came walking by us along with a man. We all kept out eyes on it, and he kept his eyes on us. It was only about twenty feet away from us, which was about as close as we had ever been to one. All of a sudden, it turned toward us and went directly at the lieutenant. Did I mention that most water buffalo have horns that span six to eight feet? He pinned our lieutenant to the ground, and it was a good thing that the ground was a little moist and soft. The water buffalo kept on driving forward like he was trying to bury the lieutenant, which in a way he was doing. Three of us on each side of the lieutenant all had our M-16 rifles in our grasp. Someone yelled, "Shoot him!"—of course they meant the water buffalo—so we all began shooting that big water buffalo. At first it got madder and started to push harder, so we kept on shooting. We all used up all our clips on this water buffalo, which meant we shot anywhere from 180 bullets to 240 bullets, depending on how full each clip was. The water buffalo finally dropped dead, which sounded like a big tree falling to the ground. The lieutenant was not hurt but was really shaken up—and who wouldn't be after having a gigantic water buffalo drive you into the ground? He still tells that story today, just like all of us who were there. I wonder how it has changed over the years from his point of view, and he did have a good point of view.

Now, the farmer stood there watching all of this take place, and I do believe that, if he had had an M-16 in his hands, he would have shot all of us. A water buffalo is the most important thing a Vietnamese farmer can have, and it is very valuable to them. He was screaming something over and over, and I didn't understand but I know it wasn't something good. We did feel bad about killing his water buffalo, but there was nothing else we could have done. I believe the farmer knew that. We collected all the money we could and gave it to him. I don't know what it would cost him to get another water buffalo, but he was very happy with the money we gave him. I don't know how he got that dead water buffalo home, but I'm certain he did because the Vietnamese people used every part of animals for something.

The spiders were something to see. Some of them were very big, and their webs spread from tree to tree. Many spiders' bodies alone were bigger than my hand. Walking point most of the time, I ran into a lot of webs, but I never did get bitten by any spiders, for which I was very thankful. When I would tell stories about spiders, I know my kids thought I was exaggerating. One day while vacationing in Florida, we were putting golf balls when something caught my eye. I could not believe it when I saw a spider web that hung between two trees that were about fifteen feet apart. We located one of the spiders, which was about the size of my hand, and I turned toward my kids with a big smile and said, "I told you."

The mosquitoes in Vietnam were everywhere, especially in the south because of all the water, swamps, and rice paddies. When things got quiet at night, we could hear them flying around, and I believe they enjoyed drinking our mosquito spray like we would drink water. The rain and wind were our friends because they kept the mosquitoes away from us. They truly did like American human blood and would drive some of the soldiers crazy. At night I always liked to have some sort of noise to go to sleep, so having the mosquitoes buzzing around my head helped me get to sleep easier. I rarely saw the Vietnamese people swatting at mosquitoes; maybe it was because we were new blood or our blood tasted better than theirs. If that was the case, the villagers probably got mad when we left and the mosquitoes started to bite them. So, when I hear a mosquito's buzz around my head today, I think of the Vietnam mosquitoes. Maybe they followed me home.

The leeches were a totally different story. Even though they were after our blood like the mosquitoes, they were more difficult to get off our bodies. We could just swat mosquitoes, and they were dead and gone, but with the leeches, we had to be more careful. We couldn't just pull them off because their bodies would separate from their heads, and their heads would remain attached to our skin. Only two things got them off the skin: heat, like from a cigarette butt, and mosquito spray. There is a very good reason they were called bloodsuckers: because that is exactly what they did. They sucked our blood. When we crossed any type of water, we always took off our uniforms afterward to check for leeches—and it seemed like we always found them. At times, we would find a lot of leeches after crossing a body of water. One person could have ten to fifteen leeches at one time, and let me tell you, they had no respect regarding where they chose to land on someone's body. I did not like leeches, and I did not like even getting leeches off someone, which I did, but I did not like even looking at leeches.

The fire ant, which I like to call the vampire ant, was the worst insect over there and the meanest insect I have ever seen. I called them vampire ants because I would watch them walk up my arm, go to my neck, and bite me there. I know this sounds like I made it up, but I saw what I saw. I was bitten on the arm and other places, but most often I was bitten on the neck. I believe I know how fire ants got their name: they would bite the fire out of you. You may wonder why I would watch an ant crawl up my arm, across my shoulder, and to my neck only to bite me, and that is a very good question. There are two reasons for this: first, it would break up the boredom when we were just sitting around taking a break or were done walking for the day. The second reason is that I wanted to see if I was just imagining the ant's strange behavior. There were many booby traps in Vietnam, and the fire ant hills were among the best. But they did provide a form of entertainment for us when one of the soldiers accidentally sat on one of those hills. We would laugh until tears fell from our eyes, and then we felt bad for him because the bites truly did hurt. At times we laughed at the strangest things, but the laughter kept us from going crazy. When all this kind of stuff was going on, I would pause and think, *How did I end up in Vietnam anyways?*

8

How Did I Get in Vietnam Anyway?

I started to think about Vietnam when I entered high school in 1965, which was the year my older sister, Pat, graduated from high school. My younger sister, Jackie, was two years behind me, so I was the middle child of the family. When I entered high school, I started to hear about guys going to Vietnam. Each year, around five hundred students graduated, and it seemed like every day some guy was getting drafted into the army. My sister's boyfriend, Don, got drafted in October 1966, which really put the war in Vietnam on my mind a lot, even though I had two years to graduate. Vietnam became the number-one news item on TV and the number-one talk in barbershops and beauty salons. Two things happened that made me think about what I was going to do when I graduated from high school at seventeen years old. The first was when Pat's boyfriend got wounded in Vietnam, ended up in Valley Forge Medical Center, and was discharged from the army after he had surgery. He later married my sister, and they have been married for fifty-four years—which is a surprise because they got married on April 1, 1967, or April Fools' Day. The second thing that happened was that one of my neighborhood friends was killed in Vietnam, which brought reality to everything about Vietnam. I could hardly believe my ears when someone told me about his getting killed; it was like a bad dream. Now, you would think this would have caused very negative thoughts about my going into the service, but I didn't think either way on it at this time. I knew the day was coming that I would have to do something. Any guy with whom I had graduated from high school who could walk and pull a trigger was drafted, especially as the war in Vietnam escalated every year.

I entered my senior year in September of 1966 with three important things on my mind: Sandy, my girlfriend; Vietnam; and myself. I cannot tell you how or why I came up with the following idea at the age of seventeen years old, but I thought of it and was going to do it. I heard that people could volunteer for the draft so they wouldn't have to wait until they were nineteen years old, the minimum age to get drafted, as mentioned in chapter 3. I was going to graduate in June 1967 at the age of seventeen, so I knew I would be drafted as soon as I turned nineteen. But I didn't want to wait to be drafted when I would have a job and most likely be married to Sandy. I didn't want to leave all that for two years, so I thought, *Why not volunteer now for the army so that, when I graduate, I can go right into the army and get it over with? Then I'll get out when I am nineteen years old and go on with my life.* Once I settled on that plan, I did not think of doing anything else but that. Hey, I would be only nineteen years old and have my service time behind me, which I thought was a pretty good idea. And it turned out to be just that. My friends thought I was crazy because their reasoning was that a lot could change between graduation and my nineteenth birthday. I did consider that, but I couldn't get the thought out of my mind that I would be nineteen years old and have my service time done, and that is what kept me pursuing this plan for my life. Two years of life seems like a very long time to give to the army, but back then people didn't think that way. I know I didn't. I wanted to do my part for my country and to stop communism from spreading to our country. It may sound corny today, but back then our country was different and people's pride in the United States was different. I know some may not get what I am about to say, but without hesitation, I would do the exact same thing again. I really do not have any regrets over the decision I made. Again, patriotism was strong back then, even with the ongoing protests, because many Americans supported the troops who fought. We may not have understood all the things that got us involved in Vietnam, but we were Americans who knew we were living in the greatest country in the world, and we were going to fight for our country.

I really believe that we as a country have lost the American spirit that was so strong back in the sixties and early seventies. America is the greatest country in the world, and I was born here and raised here, for which I am so thankful. Of course, Vietnam was a political war. It is a shame that the politicians did not let the generals conduct the war, as it would have been over years before it ended. That part I did not like, but I still believe this is the greatest country in the world and would defend it today. Okay, that is my rant. I really am thankful that I am an American citizen and live in the best country ever.

9

The First Bullet
Fired at Us

Like I wrote in chapter 5, we came up empty handed after our first week in the bush looking for the VC, which was okay with us. The only problem with that is that we started letting our guards down and becoming relaxed, saying, "Well, this is not so bad after all. What was I scared about anyways?" After a few days at base camp, we headed out for our second time in the bush looking for the VC. I believe it was the second or third day out when we had our first encounter with the enemy—a sniper who fired at us. Most of the time, snipers would sit in the trees because they had a good view of troops walking around. They knew all the best spots to be to get that good shot at us. By the time we hit the ground, got settled, and started looking for them, they would be out of the tree and heading for the next spot to shoot at us. Sniping wasn't their most effective way of hurting us, although every once in a while they would hit someone. It was mainly to scare us, annoy us, and anger us, and at times it was successful. So after that first encounter with the enemy, we felt like we were true veterans of the war. Little did we know that was not the case.

The booby traps were the next thing to look out for, and they were nothing like the booby traps in the north of the country. The water in our area made it hard to create very many traps, but the north had more dry land. I only heard about some of their booby traps, which sounded awful, and I was glad they were not around us. Punji pits and wired hand grenades were the two most common traps for which we had to watch out. The VC made the punji stakes from bamboo, set them in a hole, and covered the tips with all kinds of matter so that, if someone stepped into the hole, he would fall in and the tips of the sticks would puncture his boots. I never stepped in a punji pit, for which I am thankful. They would slice through the bottom of a soldier's boot and into his foot, and the stuff on the spike tips would infect him. The water in the Mekong Delta really hindered the success of these booby traps because the water was everywhere. This did not stop the VC from putting them out, however, because they knew they would get someone. They did, but not many.

The closest encounter I ever had with a booby trap was a very scary moment for me. We were on a night mission, which I hated because I couldn't see a thing around me. I was walking ahead of the rest and felt a wire hit my leg. Knowing immediately that it was a booby trap, I jumped to the ground and yelled, "Trap!" I put my hands over my head and eyes, waiting for the next sound. The story was that no one ever hear the sound of the explosion or bullets hitting them, so I knew that if I heard the bullets or the explosion, it would mean that I was okay and not hit. I really do not know how long it was before anyone moved, but like always, it seemed like a long time. I finally started to move and get my flashlight out. Again, this is why I didn't like going out at night—I couldn't see a thing. I started to look around to see what was going on and if I could find the booby trap. My leg did touch the wire, and that was supposed to set off the trap so the trap was somewhere close to me. I finally found it; it was an old, rusted hand grenade, but the pin had not come out because of the rust. Oh, yeah, one small detail—the hand grenade was about one foot from my head. Yes, I said one foot. With my voice shaking and in a very high pitch, I said, "I found the trap." There is no doubt that it was not my time to go. It goes without saying that if the trap had gone off, you would not be reading this book. I was not a religious person at that time, but I did thank God for saving my life. Soldiers often got religion at times like this, in firefights, when someone near them was shot, and when they were shot themselves. We slowly, very slowly picked up the grenade and buried it as deeply as we could because we did not want an innocent person getting hurt, especially the local children, who liked playing with things like these.

As I look back and think about all the times a soldier has escaped death, it seems overwhelming. I watched a big old guy beside me drop to the ground as his helmet went flying off his head. I thought for sure he had gotten shot in the head and was either dead or a mess. After a few moments, he got to his knees, looked at me, and said, "What happened?" I didn't see any blood, so we both were puzzled. I had seen him drop and had seen the helmet fly like a bird landing about fifteen feet from us. I picked up his helmet and helmet liner, and I couldn't believe my eyes—I saw a bullet hole in the front of his helmet and another on the side toward the back. The bullet had gone between his helmet and helmet liner and exited out the back. He didn't even get a scratch. Of course, he ended up with a huge headache, but he didn't mind that too much. The sad thing was that there were way too many stories of people who they didn't make it or were badly wounded.

It seemed that, after our first encounter with the enemy, we were always subjected to some sort of attack when we went out. The war was definitely getting worse, and the enemy was escalating its efforts to eliminate us. We didn't realize it at the time, but the Tet offensive was getting closer and closer, which meant the enemy was going to go for the gusto and do whatever it could to overrun us. It started in January, and I am not sure when it ended, but it was a very rough time in Vietnam. The VC attacked the US Embassy in Saigon, which served as a short-time R&R (rest and recuperation) stop for Americans. It was a very nice place, I was told. After it was attacked, my group was sent to Saigon to help protect the embassy and the city. When we arrived there, the city was a mess. Dead bodies and running people were everywhere. The VC was also everywhere, firing at us from every direction, which made it hard to find shelter. We ended up in stores or office buildings or wherever we could find to protect ourselves. I have not said it for a while, but I had graduated from high school just six months earlier and had been playing war in my safe backyard with my toy soldiers and tanks six years earlier, and now I was going through the real thing with real bullets. Wow. It is truly amazing how the human mind works. I got used to seeing awful and gross things, and they didn't bother me like they used to. We would stop for lunch or just to rest in an area with dead bodies everywhere, and we would just talk and eat like it was no big thing. I remember sitting down to eat lunch while watching all kinds of fighting going on across the river, like I was watching a war movie on TV during supper. The things I saw in Vietnam are the type that could consume a person for the rest of his life if he let them. There is no way to ever forget them, but I did manage to let them go so I can go on. So if you are a Vietnam veteran or a veteran from another war, please get help and start letting go so you can live a good life, which you deserve. I know you can because I have done that, and I am nobody special, just an infantryman who carried a radio walking point during the war in Vietnam.

Riding an airboat was fun and another way for me to escape from the war. I only rode on them a few times, but they could go anywhere and get there fast. It was another amusement park ride for me.

Our sleeping quarters were always interesting. We were resting and staying out of the sun. I was the one without shoes. It always felt good to take off those army boots. It is amazing how fast I could put those boots on when a firefight started.

Friends in Vietnam Never Forgotten

I met a lot of guys in boot camp and advanced individual training, but the relationships I developed in Vietnam will never leave me. If you can, imagine the time we spent together for one year in all kinds of situations. One day we would sit around talking about our favorite football teams and laughing at a bad joke, and another day we would be trying to keep one of those soldiers alive or, worse yet, watching him die. Remember when I wrote about a soldier getting that "Dear John" letter? Well, guess who the only person he could talk to about it was. Maybe me or another soldier. I believe this is why soldiers mature faster in life. These are some heavy-duty things that take place in people's lives. I had just turned eighteen years old a few months earlier, and suddenly I was trying to help a soldier who was thinking about ending it all because his wife left him and took his children. I have tried to help soldiers who were so depressed because they never got any mail or their wives were having their first babies while they were thousands of miles away and would not see their children for months. I could go on and on with all the counseling sessions I had with other soldiers at the ripe old age of eighteen. The bonds created with these guys are as tight as they get. But it wasn't always the hard things that brought us together; the funny things that happened did the same. Sometimes we would laugh so hard at the craziest things that our guts would hurt for hours. I found out that laughter was a very good thing, so I tried to keep my buddies entertained. I have said this before, but I do have a strange sense of humor. The Bible tells us that a merry heart is like medicine, and I know that is true because I saw laughter work on hurting soldiers.

I would like to interject something here about my wife, Sandy. I saw many good soldiers get shot by bullets and then recover to live a normal lifestyle. I also saw many good soldiers get shot in the heart by a "Dear John" letter, and some of them never recovered from it. I will never understand why a woman would not wait until a man got home to leave him. He was thousands of miles away in a war fighting for his life and didn't need outside distractions. I think of Sandy waiting for me even though she was only eighteen years old also. She had to mature quickly too, and she did. She remained faithful to me the whole two years I was in the service, and I am so grateful for that. There were times in Vietnam when knowing Sandy was waiting for me until I returned was the only thing that kept me going, and some guys had that hope taken from them.

The friendships developed in Vietnam last forever, even if we never saw one another again, which was mostly the case. The hardest time was when one of our brothers got killed or critically wounded and we never saw them again. I really didn't think that way at the time, but when I stopped and thought of the bond I had with that soldier, it hit me. Many good friends of mine made the ultimate sacrifice for our country—their lives. I developed friendships with many soldiers who were killed or badly wounded, and I didn't know how to react because I had never gone through anything close. This is one thing we are not trained for—that hurt that penetrates deep into your heart for a soldier who was just killed or badly wounded in front of you. It is hard to explain that feeling to anyone. How could I explain what it feels like to see a friend get shot right in front of you or get wounded so badly that his scream could be heard from far away? We had to toughen up or crumble when this happened, and most of the time we hardened ourselves to it, which was the only way to survive. Believe me when I say that there were times, mostly when I was alone, that I cried so hard about seeing my good friends die that I got sick.

I think a lot about the other guys who made it home and wonder how they are doing because we never did exchange addresses, though I don't know why. I have heard of some outfits that still get together today, and I wish we could do that because I believe it would be great to talk with them without having to worry about getting shot. I wonder how Rodriguez is doing because, the last time I saw him, he was waiting for the helicopter to come take him to the hospital after getting his legs blown off. I can think of so many guys I haven't seen since Vietnam and wonder how they have lived their lives. It is so strange; you can't get any closer to a person than fighting for your lives together, and suddenly you don't see them again.

One of my soldier friends and I did exchange addresses. I still don't know what prompted us to do that, but I am sure glad we did. Robbie is from Indiana, and we developed a very close relationship while we were in Vietnam. We have watched our children grow up and have exchanged stories about being dads and then grandfathers and even great-grandfathers. Robbie and I have been so good for each other all these years after Vietnam, which has been a blessing for me. We have battled this thing called life together, and it has not always been easy. We both have cancer, which is like a sniper firing at you and hitting you. You don't see him, but you feel his results. I believe the reason Robbie and I hit it off so well in Vietnam is that we both had a good sense of humor, even in the most difficult times. Robbie, thank you for all these years of friendship and encouragement and, yes, your stupid jokes that have helped me through Vietnam and the rest of my life. It is my privilege to have called you my friend for over fifty years and to have had you to put up with me and my stupid jokes.

In the battles you go through in this life—and there are many—stay close to your friends and never stop being a friend. Good friends will help you through the battles. The Bible tells us in Proverbs 18:24, "A man that hath friends must shew himself friendly: and there is a friend that sticketh closer than a brother" (Proverbs 18:24). Look around and develop good friends who will help you through the battles of life. I know some will turn on you or let you down, but keep the ones who stick with you close and be a friend to them.

To all my great friends while I was in Vietnam, thank you for helping me get through those hard times. To that sergeant from New York, thank you. To that soldier from California, thank you; we watched James Brown entertain the troops together. To that soldier who would never wear clothes while at the base camp and kept us laughing, thank you. To that soldier who would entertain us with his awful singing, thank you. To that soldier who never stopped talking about how beautiful his wife was, and she was, thank you. To that soldier who would laugh at anything and get us to do the same, thank you. To that soldier who was always talking about how good God was in everything, thank you. To that soldier in the hospital who taught me how to shuffle player cards, thank you. To that doctor in the hospital who was always so positive with me, thank you. To the medic who never left me and was sent from God for me, thank you. To that soldier who tried to teach me to play the harmonica even though I never got it, thank you. To all the soldiers who gave their lives in Vietnam, I thank you and salute you. To all the soldiers who were a huge part of my life in Vietnam, thank you for everything and for helping me.

The War in Your Mind

By February in Vietnam, we had seen a lot of firefights since we took that first sniper round over three months earlier. I had seen things no person should see at all, much less in one lifetime. I came to the conclusion that, without a doubt, a soldier's worst enemy in Vietnam was his mind, not a physical enemy. I knew that the VC could kill or badly wound soldiers, but I also knew that those soldiers' minds could do the same. Some soldiers went home from Vietnam without a scratch on them, but their minds were badly wounded or even killed from the war. Soldiers' minds are always going through things that they are fighting with. When one of their buddies gets killed, they think about how that could have been them or how that buddy's family and friends will react when they get the news. When a buddy is critically wounded and gets shipped back to the States, those still fighting the war think about how this is going to affect them from then on. Their minds put them through the *what ifs*. That thought was always in my mind, but I couldn't keep it there because it would drive me crazy. I believe my fight with my mind was easier for me at the time because of my age and sense of humor. The mind could make people do strange things in Vietnam because they were always thinking about something. They were involved in a war almost every day, so that is where their minds were most of the time.

I once saw a soldier shoot himself in the foot to get taken out of the field. I know this does not make any sense, but the mind will make people do things that are not normal—and believe me, we were not in a normal situation. Some soldiers killed themselves because walking around to find someone to kill or getting ready to be killed was too stressful. This is the hardest thing about being in Vietnam to deal with; as I said before, we saw things that no one should see. Even today, I can smell something like diesel fuel, and my mind will take me to Vietnam because that is all we smelled while living on the ships when we worked with the navy. I can hear a loud explosion like fireworks or a car backfiring, and my mind takes me back to Vietnam because we heard a lot of loud noises like that. I can burn myself and smell my flesh burning, which is an awful smell, and see the small kids who burned to death in a village that was just bombed. People's minds can be their greatest enemies or their greatest escape from their enemies, if that makes any sense.

As you are reading this, it may be hard to imagine that this could never happen to you, but until you are walking in those shoes, or army boots, you don't know how your mind will react. I once saw a big, strong soldier just freeze up, as stiff as a board, out of fear of what he had just seen. Medics put him on a stretcher, and he was taken by helicopter to a hospital, not because of a flesh wound but because his mind took him someplace. And I never saw him again. Imagine that you are thousands of miles away from your family, friends, and safe surroundings, and now you are in war shooting at people and getting shot at even though you don't know these people. The one to whom you could tell all your troubles or just vent what was on your mind just got killed or critically wounded, and you will never see that person again. Your mind immediately goes to, *Now what am I going to do?* Imagine you see one of your brothers get so badly wounded that he is screaming and rolling all over the place, and you watch the medic trying to settle him down while patching him up, and your mind is racing. It's just what happens. Even now, I will be watching a football game when one of the players gets badly hurt, and the cameras show him rolling around while the other players watch the team doctor try to settle him down and ease his pain, and some of the other players may be crying or praying—yes, sometimes my mind will take me back to Vietnam because I saw that scene there many times. While I was in Vietnam fighting with the VC, my mind would take me back home, where I was watching a movie with Sandy and not thinking about whether I was going to die or get wounded.

Your mind can be your very best friend or your worst enemy, which I know sounds crazy but is true. Knowing this can save your life because no one else can control your mind like you can. I do not like having an MRI done—the inside of that tube is not a good place to be for forty-five minutes—but I will go someplace else in my mind, like a beach, or I will sing along with the music and have my mind take me to a safe place. It is important to control your mind in bad situations, like Vietnam or whatever it may be. About three years ago, a friend of mine asked me to join him and his friends to go shooting, so I said, "Sounds like fun." We were in this big, open backyard, and we started shooting different types of guns and rifles. Sometimes we were all shooting at the same time, and suddenly my mind took me back to Vietnam and I started to feel funny. I had to leave. I know the guys felt bad that I was feeling this way, but my mind took me there. I could have fought with my mind and stayed, but this was one time I thought the best thing to do was leave. So I believe I won that battle.

Another time, I went hunting with a friend of mine a few months after I was discharged from the army, about six months after I got out of Vietnam. I thought I would be okay. He walked in the woods as I walked on the outside of the woods, and he kicked up a rabbit and took a shot at it. I could not see him, but I heard the shot, dropped to the ground, and aimed my shotgun toward the sound of the blast, which meant toward my friend. I laid there for a few minutes thinking about what I had just done. My mind had taken me back to Vietnam, and I had done exactly what I did there—I was trained to survive. I yelled at my friend, and once he came out of the woods, I told him what had happened. What happened next was kind of funny—funny to me but not him. In a slow, deliberate voice, he said, "Tom, give me your gun." I told him I was okay and that I had just gone back to Vietnam mentally. He looked me directly in the eyes and said it again, more slowly and deliberately: "Tom, give me your gun." Again, I told him I was okay and the thought had passed. I tried to reassure him, saying, "Really, I am okay. It was just one of those things. I should have not gone hunting this soon, but I am okay." For the third time, he stared into my eyes, and I think I saw some fear in them this time. "Tom, please, give me your gun." I could see that this could go on forever and that he was not going to stop because he was hunting with a Vietnam veteran who had just gotten out of Vietnam where he was shooting at people. It did register with me what he must have been thinking; remember, your mind takes you a lot of places. So I gave him my shotgun. We didn't talk too much on our walk back to his house, but he never did ask me to go hunting with him again, which I totally understood. It is amazing how your mind can take you somewhere in a split second, and it seems so real, like you're there. I am so glad and thankful that I have had only a few experiences like this because I know some Vietnam veterans who struggle with this more regularly. I believe what has helped me is that I have always talked about my time in Vietnam and kept my strange sense of humor. I truly feel bad for the soldiers who have a hard time getting their minds out of combat or getting past what they saw in combat. Soldiers will never forget what they have done or seen in combat, but they can let go of it. There is a big difference between forgetting and letting go, but I do know the power of the mind. A year in Vietnam can control your whole life if you let it. I have talked to many Vietnam veterans who have problems related to their experiences there, and at times I just don't know what to say or do to help. My hope is that this book will be some sort of help to all the veterans who are having trouble coping with life. I want every veteran to have a joyful and peaceful life, which I know is possible.

12

My Valentine's Day Gift

In Saigon, we were trying to protect our embassy and the city. At times, we would go right into the city, and at other times, we would stay on the outskirts. Even though the fighting had become more intense, I still really thought I would never get shot. I don't know if the other soldiers thought the same because we didn't talk about it. We didn't know that the Tet offensive was going on, either; all we knew was that the fighting had increased and more soldiers were getting shot. It was Valentine's Day, February 14, and I was walking point along with two other guys on the outskirts of Saigon when we spotted some VC. Then they spotted us and started to run. We ran after them, which was always an adventure while carrying the radio and other stuff I had on my back, but I was in pretty good shape. Today, carrying the groceries to the house while walking is a major feat today, but let's not go there. As we chased the VC, we lost them all of the sudden, which happened a lot because they knew the area and the hiding places. But this time was different because they wanted us to chase them so they could trap us, which they did. There was water ahead of us, and they surrounded us; it was a horseshoe trap, but of course we did not know this at the time. It was a hard chase, and we, mostly meaning me, were very tried so we took a little rest. When I rested, I looked for a tree or something to rest the radio on. I also took the weight off my shoulders, which really felt good, especially after a run like we had just done. It took the pressure off my neck, which at times would get pretty sore, so this was a favorite time for me. I sat there, most likely thinking about Sandy, my family, and my friends, wondering what they were doing back home that day. Even thinking about home felt good because I had been home a few months earlier but now I was in Vietnam, running around some dense jungle, and hunting for people someone called our enemies, who were guys like us hunting for their enemies, who were us. It sounds strange, but it is war and I was in the thick of it. As I sat there, I heard a *zig zig* go past my head, and I knew that is not a good thing to hear so, instead of just staying behind the tree, I did something that was not very smart—I turned around to see who was doing all the shooting. I did not know at the time that this was a very bad idea because I had been perfectly safe behind that big tree. I reacted as if I were back home leaning against a tree while hunting for rabbits, but of course I was not. I can only imagine what the VC thought when I stuck my big head out from behind the tree. As I said before about carrying a radio, it was the number-one target for the VC to shoot at. I was that target, so when they saw my head poke around that tree, they increased their firing. What I am about to explain is something I never thought could happen, especially to me—hey, I will never get shot. One of the bullets hit the ground and ricocheted, hitting me in the jaw, going through my mouth, and ending up in my other cheek. The VC kept shooting and hit my radio twice, which started me spinning. When the spinning stopped, I was lying on my stomach, looking at the tree I had just been sitting against a few seconds earlier. I really had no idea what had just happened, but I heard my buddies starting to yell for a medic because they had seen the whole thing. It must have been a sight to see, and I know they are still telling their grandkids about this radio man spinning in the air.

Now, the body does some amazing things, and I discovered one of them at this time. I did not feel a thing and never blacked out. At times like this, the body goes into shock, and that is different for everyone. I have seen soldiers go into shock and become stiff as a board. I have seen soldiers lose their legs or arms and not even realize it, and I have seen soldiers feel the pain right away and just start screaming and rolling around. I watched our medic as he ran around helping wounded soldiers even though he had bullet holes along with other wounds himself. I have seen guys get so mad that they would throw something or just yell, and I have also seen soldiers laugh after seeing that they were shot. So I don't know how all that works, but in my case, I did not feel a thing. I just lay there wondering who had been hit. However, we were now in a major fire fight in this horseshoe trap. The VC was surrounding us, which was not a very good thing, needless to say. As the guys continued to yell for a medic, I felt something on my chin. It felt warm, so I wiped it away—and then I saw the blood on my hands. I really do not know what I thought at the time, except I did know one thing: it was me who had been hit, and I must have been hit in the head. So all this yelling for a medic because someone was hit was for me. I started to yell for a medic along with my buddies, but when I did, my mouth opened and the stuff that started to come out was not pretty. I lost about 50 percent of my lower jaw and nine teeth, all of which started to come out. The next thing that happened was amazing: the bullet come out of my mouth, and I caught it with my hand. I spit the bullet out. I did not know how significant this was until I got back to my unit, which I will explain later. My medic was from Mexico, and I called him the mad Mexican because he would get mad when one of us would get hit. We were close because he liked my strange sense of humor and I made him laugh. He came over to help me, and my mind started to wander and think of all kinds of things as he wrapped my head up. *How do I look?* and *How bad am I shot?* were my thoughts, but I had one more big thought. Before I started to swell, I was able to talk a little and asked my medic, *Will I still be able to kiss Sandy when I get back home?* He started to laugh and said, "Yes, you will be able to kiss Sandy again." I really didn't believe him because I had just watched bones and teeth come out of my mouth along with the bullet. There was a moment when our eyes locked onto each other's. Neither one of us said a thing, but for some strange reason, I saw something in his eyes that made me feel like it would be okay. He finished wrapping my head, leaving an opening for my nose and mouth. He told me I had a million-dollar wound, which meant I would be going home. Now that made me feel really good. I still hadn't seen how bad I was and still didn't feel any pain—until about an hour later. The pain I started to feel made up for all the pain I had not felt at first. The firefight we were in became very intense, and I started to wonder, *Are we going to get out of here alive?* We ended up losing about nine soldiers, and eleven were badly wounded, including me.

The army was able to call in air strikes, which took care of most of the VC, but not all of them. The firing did stop for a while, allowing everyone to settle down a little, but it also made us realize what had just happened. I could hear soldiers moaning and crying out in pain. I looked behind me and saw one of my buddies with both of his legs gone. I still wonder how he is doing. I know this may sound crazy to even think about, but I started to get mad at myself. What was I thinking, turning around instead of just sitting behind that tree where I was safe? The thought still comes to my mind every once in a while, but it is what it is and no thought will ever change that. I will explain later on why I am grateful that this happened to me. That sounds strange, but it is true. Remember, it was Valentine's Day, and I would be getting my Purple Heart.

I will never forget the day I was shot. I can remember those six years earlier when I played in my backyard with my toy soldiers. When I would shoot one of the other soldiers, I would make him roll around and I would even scream out loud. How could anyone have known that I would be seeing all the things I had played out in my backyard taking place in real life? I would play for hours and would always win, so I applied that thought to this time of my life: *I am going to win. I will not let this very serious time of my youmg life ruin the rest of my life.* So from the very moment that I first talked to someone, my medic, I made him laugh with my question about kissing Sandy again. I have not changed my strategy. I learned it from my dad. After our house burned to the ground, we were all sitting around my grandparents' home with only the clothes on our backs. My dad walked in, and his very first words were, "If we only had some hot dogs, what a time we could have had!" This was one of the worst things we went through as a family, and joking was his way of getting through it. And it worked on us. It is what I said in chapter 12—your mind can hurt you or help you. It depends on where you take it and how long you stay there.

13

Wounded and Going Nowhere

All of the wounded soldiers were put in one spot so that the medic had an easier time taking care of us. So, there I was with soldiers with all types of wounds laying around, and I thought, *What just happened? I just graduated from high school a few months ago, and now I am in Vietnam with my head all wrapped up, laying with soldiers who have all kinds of wounds to their bodies.* It finally hit me like no other time—*I just got shot in the mouth. How could this have happened? I thought I would do my year in Vietnam and go home and that would be it.* Another thought came to mind: *You are alive. Nine soldiers are not alive.* Using another radio, a soldier called in a helicopter, which used to be my job. The unwounded soldiers lined us up in order of wound severity so we would be first to get on the first helicopter, and I was in that first group to go. I do not remember how many were with me, maybe four or five. When the helicopter started coming down, heavy gunfire was directed toward it. We managed to get on the helicopter and it started to lift up, but one of the enemy rounds hit something that made the helicopter come down. It couldn't go on. We had to get off the helicopter and stay there until the next day because the situation became too dangerous for another to come. We hoped it would be safe then to land a helicopter. Remember when I wrote that the worst enemy you have is your mind? Well, my mind started to think of all kinds of things. I'm sure the other wounded soldiers were thinking the same thing. I wondered how bad I really was because it hadn't been very long since I spit bones and teeth from my mouth. And yes, I wondered if I would really be able to kiss Sandy again and if my whole face was a mess and whether I would ever look the same. *Will Sandy think I am too ugly and not want to be with me anymore? Will my friends laugh at me?* I know this does not make any sense, but as I have already said, your mind can truly wound you.

The night took a long time to give way to morning, but I will admit that I was not in any pain thanks to that mad Mexican medic who told me, "You will not be in any pain." He kept giving all the wounded soldiers pain medicine, which was a blessing because one of the soldiers stayed there overnight with no legs. But he made it. I believe that none of us slept a minute that night. The morning came, a helicopter came down, and this time we made it out of the field. We were headed to Long Binh Hospital. When we arrived, the scene reminded me of the TV series *MASH*. Some guys met us at the helicopter and put us on stretchers, and off we went into the hospital. I heard the same questions over and over: "How do you feel?" and "Where does it hurt?" By this time, I was really swollen and could not talk at all, so I shook my head or rolled my eyes to indicate my answers. I wanted to say, *Hey, I just got shot in the mouth and watched bones and teeth fly out of my mouth along with the bullet. How do you think I feel? And it hurts underneath the wrapping.* I know they meant well, though, and I would probably would have asked the same questions.

Sandy had sent me some boxer shorts with hearts all over them for a Valentine's Day gift about a week before this happened. I got shot on Valentine's Day, which meant I was wearing those shorts when I got hit. So when the nurses and staff put me on the table, they began to cut my clothes off and saw my shorts. They all started to laugh and called all the others over to see me lying there in my underwear with hearts all over them. So I was the hit of the hospital and put a smile on their faces. I bet they are still talking about that when Valentine's Day comes up. I am sure they were not to supposed to laugh at wounded soldiers, but this was probably good for them because all they had seen was a steady stream of wounded soldiers, especially during the Tet offensive. Oh yeah, I still have those shorts today, and I can still get them on. It is a little harder though; I believe they shrink over time.

The picture is me right before we went out on that mission. I had made my buddies laugh when I said I was going to wear those boxers because I knew we would be in the field on Valentine's Day. But I obviously did not know I was going to get shot.

The nurses and doctors kept telling me that I was going to be all right. I knew I was going to be all right, but what I wanted to know was how I looked. The doctor took my wrapping off and said, "This doesn't look too bad." I knew he was lying; he just was trying to make me feel good. After he looked at my face and cleaned me up, he had me open my mouth, and I saw the look on his face. It was not a good look, so I started to get a little scared about what had happened to me and what the inside of my mouth must have looked like. The doctor did some cutting, snipping and stitching in my mouth, which didn't make me feel any better about my situation. I was thinking about everybody back home getting the news about my getting shot in the mouth, and I wondered if they would wonder about how I looked. It doesn't sound very good when you hear it.

When I started to think about all that had happened to me over the last two days, I started to cry and could hardly stop. The only reason

I stopped was because my mouth was really starting to hurt. I started to think about how this was going to change my life; I knew it would somehow. I was lying on a hospital bed in Vietnam at the ripe old age of eighteen, I had just been shot in the mouth, and I didn't know the extent of my injury.

I used to watch war movies at home and see guys get wounded, come home, and then act differently because of the injury. I knew they were just movies, but now I was in the movie, I did get wounded, and I would be going home. *Will I be a changed person when I get home?* I wondered. I really did not know the answer, but I didn't think I would change because of this. A lot of thoughts were running through my mind. How things change in five short months, from being in boot camp to a hospital in Vietnam.

The pictures below are of me while in boot camp and while walking around the hospital, which I did a lot once I was able. The hospital clothes were a real fashion statement. There is about a five-month difference between these photos, but about twenty years of growing up took place during those five months.

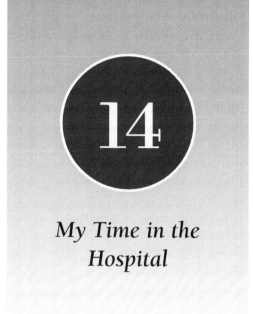

My Time in the Hospital

After the nurses and doctors stopped laughing at my heart-covered shorts, they sent me to a bed in the hospital for head wounds. I was still wondering what I looked like, which made my imagination go all over the place. I kept asking when a nurse or doctor would come by, "How do I look?" Their answer was always the same: "Not bad." I knew they were not telling me the truth. I remembered those war movies in which the wounded soldier would ask how he was doing or how bad it was, and they would always say the same thing, "Not bad." And then when the soldier wasn't looking, the doctor would shake his head. I didn't trust what they all were saying. I knew I was a mess because if the inside my mouth was that messed up, the outside must be worse. I must say, the worst ordeal I went through was when they took out the roots of the teeth that had been knocked out. I saw the doctor walk into the room with a hammer and a chisel, and I mean that. When a doctor tells you "This may hurt a little" even after shooting two quarts of pain medicine into you, you know it will be a long day. Nine teeth had been shot out of my mouth, and the roots of all nine teeth were still in my mouth. Even though a lot of my jaw was gone, those roots are deep. I may have passed out twice during the process; it seemed that the doctor asked me twice, "Are you okay now?" and "Can I continue?" Most of the teeth that had not been shot out were either cracked or chipped, which is the reason I had many dentist trips in my future.

At one point, the doctor asked me a big question: "What do you want me to do? I can pull all your teeth out now, or I can repair the ones that need it, which is about all of them." I was an eighteen-year-old kid who had just gotten shot in the mouth, and I had to answer a huge question like this. I told him I was going to write to my dentist back home and see what he wanted me to do. which took about two weeks to get his answer. He told me to save whatever teeth they can save, so that is what we did.

I finally got enough nerve to see how I looked, so I went into the bathroom and took off my bandages. I kept my eyes closed for a long time—well, it seemed like a long time. When I saw my face, I was shocked, not because of how bad I looked but because of how good I looked. I had a scar only of about one and a half inches. Ninety percent of the damage had been done on the inside; when the bullet entered into my jaw, it started to spin, causing all the damage. I truly felt a lot better after I looked at myself because I had thought my face was going to be a mess. I know it sounds crazy because, even if my face had been a mess, I would have been okay because I was alive. Many parents, wives, children, and friends would have been happy to have their soldiers come home with messed-up faces instead of not at all. The ward that I was in was for head wounds, and the strangest one, besides mine, was a tank driver who was yelling out a command and got shot in the cheek. The bullet had gone in one side and come out the other, without hitting his tongue or teeth. He has told that story over and over, like I have told mine. I thought about what one doctor had told me: if the bullet had gone a sixteenth of an inch in either direction, I would have not made it. It was a well-placed bullet that went exactly where it had to go without killing me.

I couldn't eat anything solid for a while, so I drank my meals through a straw. It was hard getting a hamburger through a straw. Just kidding, or am I? After a week of that, I started on a soft diet and finally started to eat solid food in very little bits. I lost about twenty-five pounds, and at the time I could not afford to lose any weight. I came out of the hospital weighing a grand total of 110 pounds—oh yeah, a monster of a man.

I thought I had better write my parents and Sandy to let them know that I was okay because I was sure they had heard about the injury. In reality, they did not know I had been hit because there was mix-up somewhere and they never received the news. I thought I would write something funny in my letter so they would know that I was okay. Again, with my strange sense of humor, this was easy to do. My mom saved that letter, and after she passed away, I found it. When I read it, I started to cry and then started to laugh. I want you all to read the letter, a letter from an eighteen-year-old kid who got shot in the mouth and was lying in a hospital bed. The letter is word for word, nothing added or taken out.

Dear Mr. and Mrs. Williams,

We regret to say that your son has been wounded in action. He was struck by a new secret weapon now being used by the red ants. We are awful sorry to say he has lost nine teeth, maybe more. Now Mrs. Williams stop your crying and please Mr. Williams don't be alarmed by anything for he is doing fine at Long Binh hospital. We are sorry to say that he will be out of action for some time, we need him in the field, but like we say that is war. Oh, yes, we almost forgot, your son, PFC Thomas F. Williams will or maybe already has received the Purple heart. Oh Yes, Mr. and Mrs. Williams, we are proud of him too. He is a fine and brave soldier. Well, we will close this letter, you know there is a war to be won and don't worry with soldiers like your son out in the field, we have it won.

General Stinger of the Red Ants

This is the letter that my parents received from me, word for word. I know it didn't make any sense to sign it from General Stinger of the Red Ants because the red ants had wounded me with their secret weapon. But hey, I was a kid who had just lost nine teeth and half his jaw and was lying in a hospital, so ease up. When my parents received this letter, they didn't know what to think at first and were trying to make sense of it. They concluded that something was not right and contacted the Red Cross, but my dad thought that maybe I had been hit because the letterhead was from Long Binh Hospital. The Red Cross got back with my parents right away and told them that I had, in fact, sustained a gunshot wound to the face and was in the hospital in Vietnam. Their hearts began to pound, and their minds went in every direction. The only thing that made them feel a little better was my letter, for which I was thankful. They called my sisters and Sandy, and then more people were going crazy, thinking about me and wondering how bad I was. Remember, when they all wrote letters to ask how I was doing, it took a week for the letters to get to me and a week to get my response. I can only imagine how long those weeks must have felt for them. I remember when my daughter, Janis, got mugged by a robber who smashed her face in with a brick, and we got the call to go up to the hospital. If we had not been able to hear from her or see her for two weeks, that would have been awful. That is what my parents, my sisters, and Sandy had to do—wait. We did start to communicate with one another, which made it better for everyone. A doctor came to see me and told me that I might have to go to Japan because my wound was not healing. I liked the idea because I had heard that when a wounded soldier goes to Japan, from there he usually goes home, and I was okay with that. When my mom heard that news, she started checking on flights to Japan—you know how moms are. A few days later, that same doctor came and told me I wouldn't be going to Japan because my wound had begun to heal.

After many days in the hospital, I was released back to my unit. I had not received my teeth and I had lost about twenty-five pounds. Look out, VC, because I was back and I was mad.

15

A Time to Reflect

By now you can tell that I am not a writer—just an ordinary guy looking back on his life. When my dad was sixty-five years old, he told me that time flies by so quickly and that the older you get, the faster it goes. He was so right; it truly goes by fast. The Bible tells us that our lives on earth are like a vapor—you see it and then it is gone. Ten quick years after my dad told me about time going fast, he went on to heaven at seventy-five years old. I am seventy-two years old as I am writing this book, which is so hard to believe. I have said many times that I had just graduated from high school about six months before going to Vietnam, and now it has been fifty-five years.

It seems like yesterday that my dad was lifting me up on the hood of his car and telling me to jump into his arms, and I did. I grew up in a small place called Richville, Ohio, where we lived right across from Timken Recreation Park, where I lived during the summer. My parents owned an ice-cream stand, the Tasti Cream, for two years, and I got to eat all the mistakes they made with the ice-cream cones. It was a very simple life we lived back then, and I do miss those years, but we had hard times like most families did from time to time. One day we were watching TV, and I saw smoke go past the front-door window and went out to see where it was coming from. I looked up and saw flames shooting out from the roof. I screamed, "The house is on fire!" and we watched our house burn to the ground, leaving us with only the clothes we were wearing. We lived in a motel for about three months as our house was rebuilt. So there were tough times, but we always got through them. I have seen many of my family, friends, and pets pass away, and one day it will be me. It may seem that I am headed for a dark place here, but it is not. I am just reflecting on my life and the reality of life. In the process of writing this book, I have seen three good friends of mine pass away. I realize that young people reading this book will think, *What is he talking about?* and I understand that thinking, but the ones over fifty are saying, "How true." The previous two chapters were about getting shot and being in the hospital, and now that was fifty-four years ago. That young teenager who sent me those Valentine's Day boxer shorts has been my wife for fifty-two years; in April it will be fifty-three years. Sandy and I were in the second grade together sixty-six years ago. I watched my two beautiful little girls grow up, they gave us seven grandkids, and the grandkids have given us four great-grandkids so far. I know that I have rambled on in this chapter, but writing this book has made me remember things in my past that I had forgotten about. So I have been reflecting a lot more since I started this book. It truly has been very good for me, and I have gotten more excited as I got farther into the book. Ever since I got shot and stopped to think about how close to death I was, I do look at my time on this earth differently than when I first arrived in Vietnam. I am so thankful for each day I have, and I try to live each day to the fullest. I never did much reflecting in my life because I really didn't have much time on this earth to reflect. My time in the hospital gave me time like I never had before because I couldn't do much but lie in that bed. I would look back on my life before Vietnam and think about what it would be after Vietnam. I didn't realize it at the time, but I was really maturing as a person. War will do that to an eighteen-year-old kid. My getting shot in the mouth made me a better person today, and I know this may be hard to understand for some people. I will go into some of this later on in the book. We all have times to reflect on our lives up to that point. It may be time spent in a hospital bed, a vacation, or just sitting on the back porch by ourselves. I believe it is good to have these times to slow us down and look ahead. I truly did a lot of reflecting lying on that hospital bed in Vietnam. Okay, enough reflecting. Let me start the next chapter when I returned to my unit.

16

Now I Am Superman

My buddies were really shocked to see me walk into our barracks. When a soldier gets wounded, especially when he is one of the first to get evacuated from the field, which I was, he usually goes either to Japan or home. So seeing me was a surprise. The last thing they had heard about me was that I had a million-dollar wound, so they thought for sure I was already back in the States. Their first questions were, "What are you doing here?" and "Why are you not home?" I was thinking the same thing and wondering what had happened because it did not make any sense. I did not have many teeth since I lost nine of them and a part of my jaw, and I had lost about twenty-five pounds. I looked different than I had a few months earlier, and I talked differently. I stuttered and had a hard time pronouncing certain words, which had not been the case before my injury. It was because the teeth had not been replaced yet and some of my jaw was missing, but even when I did get the bridge, I still had those problems and still do today.

One other thing happened because of my gunshot wound: I started to develop a fear of getting shot again. I didn't fear it too much before, but something happens after you do get shot. Having that much fear when out in the field is not a good situation. I really tried to fight that fear, but it was strong; even my sense of humor had a time with it. So this is where my war of the mind truly came alive for me personally. It was a battle that I had to fight hard to get through, and I did most of the time. I had a true understanding then of why some of the guys were so scared that it really did affect them in most areas. A few times, it affected me out in the field when I heard that *zig zig* going past my head; it took me right to the place in my mind where I got shot.

When brand-new soldiers would come to our unit, the guys would always ask them, "Do you want to see Superman? He's in our outfit. He catches bullets in midair and then spits them out. He is the Superman of the ninth infantry division." I knew they were looking for a six-foot, eight-inch-tall soldier weighing about 250 pounds, so I would stand up and the guys would say, "There he is—our Superman." Some would start to laugh, others were stunned, and some didn't believe it. Then I would tell them my story, and they would stare at me and ask, "Why are you not home with a wound like that?" I was beginning to ask that same question a lot myself. So my nickname changed from "the kid" to "Superman," which I was beginning to like. Sometimes when I sat in the barracks alone, I would think, *I really did spit that bullet out of my mouth,* and then I would start to shake, hearing the doctor say, "If that bullet would have gone a sixteenth of an inch in either direction, you would be dead." But hey, I am Superman. The other guys would ask me all kinds of questions about how it all happened. I believe this was another reason I was so open about everything that happened—because of all the interactions I had with my brothers.

Evidently my lieutenant liked me being on the radio because he gave it to me right before we went on a night mission. I remember like it was yesterday how I felt with that radio on my shoulders, walking around in the bush at night. A few days went by, and at one point I got a piece of scrap metal in my shoulder. It was not a very big wound; I didn't even call for a medic and didn't tell our lieutenant about it. But it did create more thoughts, like, *The next time I might not be so lucky.* I wasn't thinking clearly when I wrote a letter telling my parents about this small wound. My dad went crazy. They didn't even know that I was back in the field, so when my dad heard this, he went right to our congressman and told him my story. Well, the congressman got mad and wrote what is called a congressional letter, stating that I should be out of the field since I had sustained a gunshot wound to the head that took out nine teeth and about 50 percent of my jaw. When I thought of it that way, I did start to wonder, *What am I doing out in the bush carrying the radio again with most of my bottom teeth gone and having a hard time talking?*

I was out in the field resting my radio on the back of a tree when we heard a helicopter coming close to where we were. It landed, and someone got out and asked, "Is there a Tom Williams here?" I told him I was Tom Williams. He asked me where my lieutenant was, and when he found him, he told him that I was being shipped back to the base camp and would be working there because they had received a congressional letter about me. My lieutenant was so mad at me, thinking I had orchestrated this, but I had no idea what was happening. I went back to the base, and then my company commander *really* started to yell at me. I found out later that getting a congressional letter was not a good thing for an outfit; it was kind of a bad mark on them. But when I really think about it, I know I should have not gone back out into the field carrying the radio.

So Superman took off his warrior cape and put on his filing-papers cape. I worked as a clerk until my time in Vietnam was up. I truly had mixed feelings about this. A part of me wanted to stay with my outfit and fight with them, but the other part wanted to get out of the field to fight no more. When I shared this with the guys at the base, they told me, "Are you crazy? Get out of here while you can." That helped me a lot. However, being in the base camp all the time did not mean I was out of danger. The VC would shoot mortar rounds into our camp about twice a week. When the siren went off, we ran to the bunkers until they stopped. At times, some would be killed or wounded from these mortar rounds coming into our camp. One time, our bunker took a direct hit, and we all ended up losing our hearing for a while. There were no real safe places in Vietnam—just some safer than others. When I am asked, "Were you on the front lines?" I reply, "There were no front lines in Vietnam." In the office, being Superman did not have as much impact as it did in my other outfit, but the guys always wanted to hear stories about what had happened while I was in the field and especially while carrying the radio walking point.

Below are a few more photos of me while I was in the field.

I went from carrying this

to filing paper and typing.

17

Leaving Vietnam, but Vietnam Never Leaves You

When people got close to their time to leave Vietnam, they started x-ing out the dates on the calendar, which is called a short-timer's calendar. The closer I got, the longer the days seemed, and during that last week, every day seemed to last a week. My emotions started going all over the place, and when I was packing up and walking to the plane that was taking you home, it seemed like I was just getting off the plane that took you there. A year had passed so quickly, but that year would always be with me and changed me forever—some good changes and some bad. When I left, I was at the ripe old age of nineteen, but I seemed a lot older to myself because I had seen and been through so much that many people never go through in their lifetimes. The war in Vietnam changed many soldiers who returned home, and some never talked about it in their whole lives. I have said it before—I have always talked about my experience in Vietnam. It helped me after I returned home, as did my strange sense of humor.

When I was days away from going home, my heart pounded harder the closer it got. I thought of the soldiers who did not make the trip home and the ones who went home missing parts of their bodies. I thought of that day when I had arrived in Vietnam, thinking I would get shot while getting off the plane; I had that same feeling getting on the plane taking me home. My mind was a mess, and my thoughts were going in every direction. A year is a long time to spend away from family and friends. It was 365 days that I had just spent in a place called Vietnam where I could have been killed on any one of those days. I thought about the innocent Vietnamese people who were not leaving and who must still think that they could be killed any day. They had been thinking that for almost twenty years.

I had the option of staying in Vietnam another three months so that, when I got home, my service time would have been completed. I thought about that for a while, but I really wanted to get back home because I had seen enough. But I told my family and Sandy that I had chosen the three-month extension so that I could get out early because I wanted to surprise them. On my last day in Vietnam, I could hardly think, and I was trying to say all the right things to the guys who were staying. I figured I would see them later or keep up with them through the years. Well, we didn't, and I know we should have. Robbie was the only one I kept up with, and as I said before, our relationship has been a true blessing.

When I got on that plane to go home, I sat down in my seat, looked around, and started to cry and laugh—sometimes at the same time. Oh, yeah. About three weeks before I left to go home, my new front teeth arrived and I started to wear them, which was a big adjustment. I was so excited when I got them because I didn't want anyone at home to see me without my teeth—I looked like Gabby Hayes. When I arrived at Oakland, California, I couldn't wait to call my parents and Sandy to tell them I would be home in about five hours. I called my mom first because everyone else was working. I told her, "I am home and in California, and I will be at the Akron-Canton Airport in about five hours." Well, you know how moms are, especially my mom. She went crazy and then started to cry and laugh, and I believe there was a little bit of screaming. Many things occurred during that plane trip home. It took five hours but seemed like days. I started to rehearse what I would say to everyone and how would I react. Would I cry a lot? Would I laugh a lot? Or would I just stand there and look at everyone? I started to look back on the year I had just spent in Vietnam and how I had almost been killed. I actually was shot in the mouth; it had not been a bad dream. I thought of all the friends I had made and how some of them did not make it back home or made it back with a lot of physical problems and mental issues.

When the plane was about to land, man, oh man, was I going crazy! Over the speaker, I heard something said that some others say they never did hear; the pilot said, "Welcome home, soldier." That meant me because I was the only soldier on that plane going to the Akron-Canton Airport. Hearing that made me cry then, and I'm crying right now as I am typing it. I never cared if I had a welcome-home parade, the high school band playing when I got off the plane, or someone clapping for me as I entered in the airport because my welcome-home celebration was waiting for me in the foyer of that airport, and that is all I cared about—my family and Sandy. I am not saying that welcoming soldiers who come home from war is a bad thing. All I am saying is that soldiers' most important welcome-home committees are their family and friends. I remembered the soldiers who never did receive any mail from home, and they probably came home to an empty airport foyer, which had to be terrible for them. I hoped a friend or neighbor told them that it was good to see them and was glad they made it home safely. I hoped a grandmother or grandfather told them that they were praying for them to return safely.

The plane landed and the door opened, and I started to walk down the steps. When I got to the bottom, I got down on my knees and bent my head to the ground. I will be honest with you—I cannot remember if I kissed the ground or not, but that was my intention. I was only thinking about seeing everyone again. I was looking everywhere for them, and I spotted my mom first. She was crying like a baby. As soon as I saw her crying, I started to cry, even though I thought I didn't have any more tears left. It seemed like I had been crying for the previous few days and especially the previous five hours. I started to hug and kiss everyone, especially Sandy. I want you to think about this meeting. I had been gone for a year and had experienced all that I went through, and I could not wait to get home. On the other side, my family and Sandy had been waiting for me to come home after all they had gone through. It was like two big trains on the same track heading for each other going sixty miles an hour. The explosion was not going to be metal hitting metal, though; it was a year full of emotions hitting everyone head on. Unlike the train, this wreck was beautiful, and I have never forgotten and will never forget it. That is why I didn't need a big-time welcome-home thing: I had something better than that. I had a big train of family and Sandy coming at me at sixty miles an hour and hitting me head-on with all the great emotions a person could have. And besides all of that, I was home. I had made it back alive! I was home, I was alive, and I was surrounded by my family and Sandy. Wow! A year had gone by, and what a year it was, but it is now my past, never to be forgotten.

I was ready to start my new life with my family and friends and—oh, yeah—Sandy! At this point I did not realize how significant a part in my life that year in Vietnam would be, but it was and still is today. Even writing this book is a result of that year in Vietnam. My time there will never leave me, and I will use it for good from now on. The main impression I left with is how great our country is, because I had spent a year in a country whose people did not have much. I will share more things about Vietnam in the following chapters that may offer a different perspective on how Vietnam affected one soldier for the rest of his life.

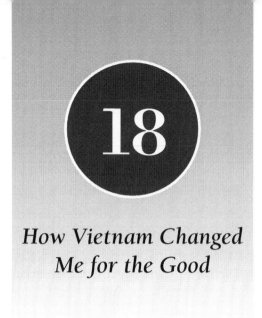

How Vietnam Changed
Me for the Good

I learned two main things in the time I have been home from Vietnam. The first is that a year goes quickly and a year goes slowly. Some moments in Vietnam progressed at a snail's pace, and other times went at a rabbit's pace; it's the same everywhere. I found out that time is a funny thing and everything revolves around it. The second thing is that, even though I was so glad to be out of Vietnam, I found out that Vietnam did not leave me. Vietnam was a stowaway in my baggage when I left, thinking I was really leaving it behind. I physically left Vietnam, but mentally I never did. I am not saying that I think of Vietnam or the things that happened there are in every moment of my life because I don't. I have thoughts of Vietnam every once in a while, but it never has controlled my thoughts or mind. Different smells and some loud noises take me back there, as do some songs. If I'm watching the news and a story about someone getting shot in the face comes on, well, of course, I will think about my wound. When I hear about orphans, I think about the children orphaned in Vietnam because of the war. When I stumble on a word I'm trying to say or stutter, I may think about Vietnam. At times, I think about the guy who shot me, and I would like to meet him. I know that sounds crazy, but I would like to have that meeting.

Listen to me: Vietnam did change me, and I know that thoughts about Vietnam are going to come up. That is normal, but like I said before, the thoughts do not change who I am. They do not dominate my life, and I will not let them. Let me give you the definition of *dominate*: to have a commanding influence on or exercising control over someone.

Vietnam did something for me for which I am very grateful. I know that does not seem possible, but let me tell you. The first thing is that I am so grateful to have been born in the United States of America. I am so much more patriotic than I was before I went to war, and I can see that I took being born here for granted. It is not perfect, but it is the best place in the world to live. I learned about third-world countries in my school history book, but until I went there and lived there for a year, I really had no idea how people there lived. I saw eight to ten people living in a fifteen-by-fifteen mud house with no running water or electricity.

The second thing that Vietnam taught me was to live each day like it could be my last. Life can change in a split second, and I saw that happen a lot in Vietnam. The change might not be felt by the soldier who was just killed, but everyone back home will feel it. Vietnam put me on day-by-day lifestyle, which is a great way to live. The third thing is that I am grateful I was shot in Vietnam. I might lose some of my readers here, but I beg you to keep reading because I will explain this further in another chapter. (I guess this is what is called a teaser.) The fourth thing for which I am grateful after being Vietnam is the food we have in the States and how easy it is to get any type of food I want at any time. When shopping for breakfast cereal in a grocery store, I see shelves and shelves of boxes of cereal of any kind, from Cocoa Puffs to Wheaties. In Vietnam, the people don't take food for granted like we do, especially in the smaller villages. Nothing went to waste in those villages, and I mean nothing. They used every part of every animal they killed for food. The strangest thing I ate in Vietnam was monkey jerky. People would slice up the monkey meat and dry it out on the roofs of their huts. One of the villagers told me to take a piece and try it. I did, and it tasted pretty good. The fifth thing for which I am thankful after being in Vietnam is the clothes that I have. In Vietnam, the people wear the same clothes over and over until they can't wear them anymore, and then they reuse the old worn-out clothes in some other way. I try not to take clothes for granted, which is hard to do today, because it seems like if we find one small thing wrong with our clothes or shoes, we go out and buy new ones. Just think about having one shirt and one pair of pants and wearing that outfit until it wore out. And it can take years for that to happen. Now don't get me talking about the running water and electricity, which were nonexistent in the small villages.

One more thing for which I am thankful after my year in Vietnam is Sandy's being faithful to wait for me that whole year. I told you about the "Dear John" letters that some of the guys got, and it destroyed some of them. It was like getting shot with a bullet. Some of them said they would have rather gotten shot with a bullet. I figured Sandy must have truly loved me because she faithfully waited for me those 365, sometimes long days. It sealed our love for each other, and it is still sealed today. I came out of Vietnam more in love with Sandy than when I left.

Yes, Vietnam has done some damage to my mind, but I truly believe that it has done more good. I realize that some may think, *What are you talking about?* But remember, I am a guy who looks at a glass and says it is half full; I am a positive type of guy. I will not let the negative things about Vietnam destroy me, so I look for the good things, which help me with the bad things. I have lived that way ever since I got off that plane at the Akron-Canton Airport in 1968.

Home and Starting
My New Life

A total of 58,220 soldiers did not come home alive from Vietnam, and around 304,000 came back wounded. It was a close one for me, but I came home alive. I thought of all the families who had been affected by Vietnam and how some of them were living their new lives. I cannot put into words how I felt about being home. I was home for about thirty days before I headed to Fort Dix, New Jersey, to finish my time with the army. So I entered the army at seventeen years old, turned nineteen in Vietnam, and was still nineteen when I was discharged. The duty at Fort Dix was pretty easy, and when the other guys found out about my being a combat-wounded Vietnam soldier, their level of respect was very elevated. That made my stay there very easy, for which I was thankful.

While I was serving at Fort Dix, I married Sandy on April 5, 1969, in Monroe, Michigan. We ran away to get married because Sandy's parents had a hard time letting go of their only child, especially to me. We got married on a Saturday, and I went back to Fort Dix that Monday. The below picture is of me standing outside of the church where we were married. And yes, I got married in my uniform.

During the last few months of my service, I drove home on the weekends. I was discharged from the army in July 1969, and I started my new life as a civilian and started looking for a job. I had the choice of many because I was only nineteen years old and had already completed my service. I started to work at the East Ohio Gas Company reading gas meters. I truly loved this job, which involved walking around, looking at gas meters, and writing down four numbers. I did this job for eight and a half years. A close friend of mine called me up and said, "I have a job for you that I know you would be good at." I told him that I had a job that I liked, but he said I would like this one too and would make twice as much money. Well, that did get my attention, so I asked him what the job was. He said, "A college recruiter for Bell and Howell Corporation." I almost hurt myself by laughing so hard, and when I got my breath back, I asked him, "Are you crazy?" I gave him eight excellent reasons that I would not take that job: First, I majored in wood shop in high school; second, I had eight and a half years at the East Ohio Gas Company, which I loved; third, I never come close to *going* to a college, let alone take classes; fourth, I didn't like change like most people, especially this big of one; fifth, after telling my family and friends, they thought I would be crazy to take that job; sixth, I didn't even own a suit; seventh, I never gave so much as an oral book report in school for fear of being laughed at; and eighth, I now stuttered and had a hard time pronouncing words. After giving that list of reasons, I thought the case would be closed. However, not only did it not close, but after talking to him some more, I said yes. That got him off my back; I knew that I would not get past the interview stage. Something was going on here that I could not see, but it showed itself.

At this point, I had been married to Sandy for almost nine years, and we had two beautiful girls about whom we were crazy, even though they drove us crazy at times. This picture shows our two daughters acting goofy, which they inherited from their father.

Sandy had been a Christian for about fifteen years, and during our first nine years of marriage, she tried to get me to church but I would not go. She even sent a preacher to our home to talk to me, but that didn't end well. I did not want anything to do with church or the Bible. I didn't have anything against church for other people, but it was not for me. I wasn't crazy about Sandy's going to church either, so she had stopped going when we started to date. I saw many Christians not acting like Christians should

79

be acting, so I would say, "What would be the use of me going to church if they act like I do?"

I went to the job interview with a newly bought suit, thinking I was really cool. I sat in the waiting room with the other guys waiting for their time, and they started to talk and ask questions, which I didn't like. One of them asked me, "What college did you go to?" I must have had a strange expression on my face as I felt drops of sweat going down my arms. I said, "I didn't go to college, and a friend of mine talked me into coming here for this interview." The room went completely silent, and the other guys couldn't even look at me anymore. I don't think they even responded to my answer. A Vietnam thought came to my mind: *What am I doing here? I shouldn't be here.* My name was finally called, and I walked into the room. The man doing the interview said, "I have your résumé and see that you didn't go to college." I replied, "That is true, and I should not be here. But if I got this job, I would give you 150 percent *because* I shouldn't be here or get this job." I left there knowing there was no way I would get the job, but it was kind of neat that I even went for the interview. I had developed a lot of courage during the year I was in Vietnam. If I could go through that year and be okay, how hard could this interview be? This is why I say that Vietnam did some good things for me.

After a month went by, I thought that my chances for the job had passed by as well. I understood that. Sandy and I hosted a New Year's Eve party at our house, and at about nine o'clock that evening, I received a phone call from a guy at Bell and Howell Corporation. He asked me if I wanted the job, and I laughed because, surely, this was a joke. He finally convinced me that it was real, and he told me to think about it for a few days. It was on my mind every second for two days. I talked to family and friends, and they still thought it was a bad idea to take the job. Sandy and I talked, and she said it was up to me and she would back me no matter what my decision was. What a great woman. I mean this from the depths of my heart. It did not make any sense to take this job, but I said yes. All of my family and most of my friends were wondering what I was doing and thought that I had just made a very bad mistake. That thought came up a lot over the next few weeks, but it wasn't strong enough to change my mind. I was twenty-eight years old, and I had just made one of the most important life-changing decisions I had ever made since volunteering for the army draft at seventeen years old. As I look back and see how going to Vietnam, being shot in the mouth, and deciding to become a college career recruiter were tied into making me who I am today, I know that I would have laughed if anyone had said this would be my path. I was being molded, and I didn't even know it.

Taking Risks

I looked back and saw that I have taken many risks that seem to be big, and they were, but I have seen a purpose in all of them so far. When I was attending high school, I didn't have a certain crowd or clique that I would hang with, although I did have many good friends. I got along with every group, whether they were the smart students, the sports people, or even the tough guys, because I didn't fall for peer pressure. I just liked people, no matter what group they were in. Even so, risk was involved because a person or two from one group seemed to always be going after another person from another group. It was a never-ending cycle of bullying. It got complicated at times, and being friends with both groups made it hard. Sometimes I needed a score card to keep up with what group was after which other group. I liked people for who they were, not for which clique they were in, but this was risky because most did not understand this kind of thinking.

It was also risky when I volunteered for the draft while a war was going on. Most people thought I was crazy for doing it, but I thought it was a good idea. The graduation class at my high school had about five hundred, and very few were going into the service. I believe I might have been the only one who volunteered.

I took many risks in Vietnam. I went into huts and buildings to make sure they were okay for my group to walk through. The southern part of the country didn't have as many tunnels as the northern part did because of the water in the Mekong Delta. But every once in a while, we would come across a tunnel, and I would go into it to make sure no VC were in there. I usually threw a hand grenade inside it. I thank the Lord that I never came across any VC while doing this. Walking point in the bush was, without a doubt, a huge risk, but I didn't volunteer for that. But oh, man, was it risky.

Taking the college recruiter position at the Bell and Howell Corporation was another huge risk. In my previous job, I talked only about 10 percent of the time. I would walk around the different neighborhoods each day, read the meters, and write down four numbers on a card at each one. But I chose to accept a job in which I would be speaking about 90 percent of the time. I went into the area high schools and spoke to juniors and seniors, sometime as many as a thousand, along with the teachers. I had never done anything close to this before, and I am still self-conscious about my speech. But I had total peace about this job—well, maybe 95 percent peace. Okay, maybe 80 percent. Sandy was also taking a big risk by backing and fully supporting me. She would be leaving a good, secure place in our lives to go into an unknown. I was responsible for the Cincinnati area, so I would leave our house on Sunday night and come back Friday night. It took me a long time to get the presentation down because I had to change words that I had a hard time pronouncing. I developed a talent for replacing words with ones I could pronounce. I got tired of the traveling, though, so another big risk came up: selling our house and moving to Cincinnati. We did and it was a change for us because we did not know anyone. Canton, Ohio, was our hometown; we knew many people and knew where all the stores and restaurants were. All of the doctors we had been to and trusted had to be left behind. We made a major change and took a huge risk moving.

I remember giving my first presentation at a high school. About four hundred students made up the audience, and I thought I was going to throw up or pass out. I did a twenty-minute presentation and really didn't remember much about it afterward. A person sure can sweat a lot under stressful conditions. I had felt this way one other time, when I went on my first mission in Vietnam and heard the guy yelling out, "Let's go! Get off the carrier!" After that first presentation, I went into some homes and signed up one student to go to Bell and Howell college. I started to like the job, but not knowing anyone around us was hard. We would go back home a lot at first, but the four-hour trip back and forth on the weekends with two small kids started to get harder and harder, so we made the trips got less and less.

I thought that when I got out of the service, I would get married, get a good job, have kids, buy a house, retire, and die peacefully in my sleep. I thought it might be that way because I had seen other families live that way, so why not me? Maybe this is why I am writing this book—because my life was not like most others. I am not saying it was special, but I know it was different. I started out as a seventeen-year-old volunteering for the draft, knowing there was a war going on. Of course, many times I would ask myself, *What have you done, Tom?* I would answer myself with the most common answer of all time: *I don't know!*

After being in Cincinnati for about a month, something was about to happen that would change my and Sandy's lives forever. I know this sounds a little dramatic, but it really is not—and I did not see it coming. If you are sixty or seventy or older, you can look back on your life and identify one or two times when something happened that changed the course of your life. Vietnam changed my life and how I look at things. At the time, I thought, *Okay, that should do it for any major things happening to me that could change me.* Well, it wasn't the last thing or even close to it, but what was coming was truly the biggest change of my life.

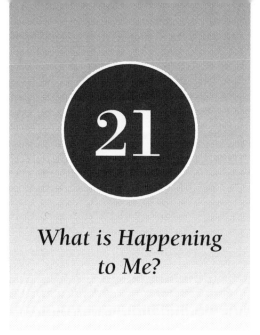

What is Happening to Me?

I went from graduating high school to army training at Fort Knox, Kentucky. From there, I went home for a month and then traveled to Vietnam, where I was a real soldier shooting at people and getting shot at for real. From the fields of Vietnam, I went to Long Binh hospital with a gunshot wound to the mouth, and then after a year in Vietnam, I went home and then to Fort Dix, New Jersey, to finish my time in the service. After that I went to work for the East Ohio Gas Company as a meter reader and then changed jobs to be a college recruiter for the Bell and Howell Corporation and moved to Cincinnati, Ohio. This all took place in about nine years, which seems long but it really is not.

A friend of mine came down to visit and stayed with us for the weekend. Something had happened to Jim a few years earlier, and he wanted to share that with me—or maybe he wanted a free place to stay. We had a good visit, and then came the question, "What do you think about God?" That is a very heavy question, and it is hard to answer. I had encountered God when I was in the Vietnam hospital and hoping not to die, so I talked to God a lot and even bargained with him about what I would do if he allowed me to live. Then, the first place I went after I arrived home was my sister's church. I walked to the front of the church and thanked God. This was my answer to Jim, which I thought was a great answer, but he didn't stop with the religious questions. He asked me,

"Why don't you go to church?" I told him I didn't want to be a hypocrite by going out partying Saturday night and then going to church the next morning. He asked me another question: "Do you think going to church is a good thing?" Well, that was a loaded question, and I knew I had to have a good answer. I said, "Of course it is." Now, I figured, that had to be the last religious question he would ask. It was not. He asked one more question: "Tom, why don't you go to church, knowing it is a good thing, and see what happens?" I didn't answer that one, but I never forgot it. I didn't realize that Sandy had been wanting to take our kids to church and was thinking about going that Sunday. Jim went home Saturday, leaving my head filled with all kinds of stuff.

October 8, 1978, a Sunday, was a day that changed my life forever. That Saturday night, Sandy had asked me if she could take the kids to Sunday school, and I said yes. She had no idea what church to go to, but she had frequently seen a church bus come into our apartment complex and pick up a bunch of kids. On the side of the bus was a church name, Landmark Baptist Church. She had no idea how to get there, and GPS didn't exist at that time; you were on your own with a map, your eyes, and prayers. I told Sandy that I didn't care if she took the girls, but I wasn't going to go. I asked her, "Where you are going to go?" and she said, "I don't know, but I guess I will follow that bus that comes here and that will take us to that church." I didn't think much about that at the time, but I wondered what that bus driver thought as he watched this car following him and stopping at each stop. Today, the police would have been called and questioned Sandy about what she was doing. Sandy and the girls ended up at Landmark Baptist Church, and she was able to get the girls into their Sunday school class. The teacher for their class was teaching the kids a song called "Jesus Loves You," a song that changed my life. Janis was three years old at the time and had an easier time learning the song than Julie, who was two years old. Let me say something here about Sunday school teachers. I know it can be hard at times because they may not be able to tell if the kids are listening, especially two- and three-year-old kids. But I want to encourage them: they *are* listening, and some of them take what they learn to a parent, sing them the song they just learned, or tell them the Bible message they heard. At home, Janis sang the song she had learned at church—three years old, blonde hair, and blue eyes, and singing to me, "Jesus loves me, this I know for the Bible tells me so." My thoughts started to go in two directions. I had named Janis after Janis Joplin, the rock-and-roll singer, because she was my favorite singer. Janis Joplin was already dead because of the drugs she took, and I thought about that as I looked at my Janis. My other thought was that the person Janis was singing about, Jesus, was someone I had heard about, but I didn't know a thing about him—not one thing. I thought about Janis Joplin and Jesus while Janis sang the song. I don't know what was happening, but I started to think about my life and where I was going with it. I was twenty-eight years old, and I had been through many things in my life, but something was missing. Everything seemed to go in slow motion as I watched Janis finish the song and go upstairs with Sandy and Julie. I dropped to my knees and asked God, "Okay, what is going on here? What are you doing?" I remembered that, while I was in the hospital in Vietnam, I had made a deal with God, telling him that if he let me live, I would live a better life. So I thought that maybe that is what this was all about. He let me live and I went on to live my life the way I wanted to, so he was telling me something. I also thought of times when I knew I was missing something and would try to fill that space with things of the world or even some sort of religion. To tell you the truth, I was a little scared, thinking, *Maybe I am having a nervous breakdown or something like that.* I finally asked God, whom I did believe in, "What do you want me to do or say?" God did not answer me, or maybe he did and I didn't recognize it. I heard Sandy and the girls coming down the steps, so I got to my feet. They came in, and I looked at Sandy and said, "Where did you go to church?" She said, "I ended up at Landmark Baptist Church and it is a real big church, but I did like it." Before I tell you what she said next, remember that this is a wife who had tried everything to get me to church. She asked me, "Why do you want to know anyways?" Now I was confused. Sandy had been trying to get me to go to church for nine years and I had not wanted anything to do with it. So her response was a little strange to me, but I did understand what she might be thinking. This had come from out of nowhere and she was not prepared for it, but neither was I. I became defensive and said, "I just wanted to know, and maybe I will go with you next Sunday." I just about knocked her over with that line, and I felt a little bit dizzy myself hearing that come out of my mouth. Sandy didn't say anything for a while; I believe she was trying to choose her words carefully because this was a very important moment going on here. She didn't want to mess up the moment by saying something that could change it.

22

A Conversation that Changed My Life

Try to think of a conversation you have had with someone that truly changed your life. How about when you proposed to your girlfriend or were proposed to? That was life changing. How about when you were going to that last interview with the person who could hire you for the dream job that you always wanted? That was life changing. How about when you went to the bank to get approved for the loan for your dream house? That was life changing. You may have had a few life-changing conversations in your life, as I have, but none of them were as big as the one I was about to have.

After Sandy told me she went to Landmark Baptist Church, she gave me the bulletin with all the information about the church. I called the phone number on the bulletin, and the pastor answered the phone. You may not think this is a big deal, but it was a very big deal. It was Sunday afternoon, and the pastor should have not been there; he should have been at a restaurant eating fried chicken by then. In fact, nobody should have been there, but he was, and I told him what had just happened to me. Pastor John Rawlings told me to get right down to the church and he would be waiting for me. I arrived at the church, and we went back to his office. I liked Pastor John from the very beginning because he didn't seem like pastor material to me, which I feel is a good quality for a pastor. He was a down-to-earth, no-nonsense guy, and I like that. I went over my story about Janis singing to me and my thoughts and prayer.

At this time, the life-changing conversation began. He started to ask me questions about my life: "Tom, have you ever been to church?" I told him I had never gone to church, even when I was younger, and our family never went for Christmas or Easter.

He asked me if I ever read the Bible, and I said, "No, I don't believe I have ever even looked inside of a Bible."

Then he asked, "Have you ever prayed for something besides your food?"

I replied, "Only once, when I was lying in a hospital bed in Vietnam and I asked God if he would let me live."

Pastor John had one more important question for me: "If you died today, would you go to heaven or hell?"

I answered, "Heaven, because good people go to heaven and bad people go to hell." At this point, I figured this was going to be the end of the questioning and I would be going home. I had told him my answer and I knew it was right, so what could be left?

He looked right at me and said, "Tom, could I read something to you from the Bible that will show you how you can go to heaven?" How could I say no, even though I already gave him the answer? He opened the Bible to the book of Romans and read this verse to me: "For all have sinned, and come short of the glory of God" (Romans 3:23). Then he asked me, "Tom, have you ever sinned?"

Of course I said, "Yes, I have. Hasn't everyone?"

He said, "Yes, everybody sins, and it is good that you recognize that you are a sinner. Remember, Tom, the Bible is God talking to us, and he is talking to you right now."

I really did not know how to respond to that, so I just said, "Okay."

He turned to another verse and read aloud: "For the wages of sin is death; but the gift of God is eternal life through Jesus Christ" (Romans 6:23). Once again, Pastor John told me that I was a sinner and must pay for my sins, and of course this got my attention. He saw the look on my face as I was thinking, *What do you mean—pay for my sins?*

He said, "But wait a minute, because someone already paid for them for you. Jesus Christ paid for your sins because he loved you so much." He then turned to another verse: "But God commendeth his love toward us, in that, while we were yet sinners, Christ died for us" (Romans 5:8). Pastor

John went on to say that Jesus Christ loved me so much that he was beaten and nailed to a cross, he died on that cross, and three days later he arose. And He did that just for me.

I was overwhelmed by then, and I really did not know what to think or say at this point. I had a lot of stuff swimming through my brain. I must tell you that I am one of the biggest skeptics around, so as I was hearing this for the first time ever, my first thought was, *How do I get out of here?*

Pastor John asked me the number-one question anyone could be asked in their lives: "Tom, do you believe that you are a sinner and that Jesus Christ died on the cross for you and rose the third day for your sins?"

It seemed like it took me twenty minutes to answer that question, but I finally said, "Yes, I do." Since I answered the question with a yes, he said he would go on. I again thought that this was over, I had answered all the questions correctly, and now it is time for me to go home.

But Pastor John said that he had one more verse to show me: "That if thou shalt confess with thy mouth the Lord Jesus, and shalt believe in thine heart that God raised him from the dead, thou shalt be saved" (Romans 10:9). I have said this before, but the next thing that to happen was going to change the course of my life. And I thought, *I have already been on way too many courses!*

Pastor John asked me, "Would you confess your sins to God and take Jesus Christ as your personal Savior and believe that he died and rose the third day for you?"

I do not know why I said yes, because I am a skeptic, but I did. Okay, surely this conversation was over and I could go home now.

Pastor John asked me, "Would you pray with me now and repeat after me the sinner's prayer? By praying this prayer, you will go to heaven when death comes your way."

How could anyone say no to this? I know I couldn't, so I said I would. We bowed our heads and closed our eyes, and I started to repeat this prayer: "Dear heavenly Father, I know that I am a sinner and I confess my sins to you. Please forgive me of my sins. I believe that Jesus Christ died for my sins and rose the third day for me. I thank Jesus Christ for coming into my heart right now. I pray this in the name of Jesus, amen."

I opened my eyes and saw Pastor John looking right at me. He said only one word: "Amen." I did not hear the Hallelujah chorus and I didn't cry or laugh. I didn't get up and run all over the place. I don't know how long I was silent, but I broke the ice by saying, "Do I have to come to church now?" He said no. That answer surprised me because I had heard that Christian people were always trying to push people to come to church. So I asked him another question: "Do I have to stop all the wrong things that I do and start doing the right things?" And again he said no. *So, I thought, I can do anything I want to do, and I still get to go to heaven. This is a great deal that I just made with God.*

Pastor John had one more thing to ask me, and it messed my thinking all up. "Tom, as much as you can, do you truly believe what you just prayed to the Lord and that it was from your heart?" I told him that I really did believe what I had just prayed or I would not have done it. Pastor John replied, "Brother Tom, you are a born-again, saved man. Now get out of my office so I can go home and get some dinner."

I looked at him and saw a silly grin on his face. I got up, gave him a big hug, and went home. Over the next year and a half, I got to know Pastor John well. He invited me to the men's luncheons, and I sat next to him. At the time, I did not realize how big of a deal what had just happened was. I arrived home and told Sandy that I just been saved. She had been praying for me for at least nine years, so this was a gigantic moment for her, but I still did not understand everyone's reaction to this. Sandy cried and kept hugging me, and she started to call all the people who had been praying for me. Once they heard the news, they started to cry and go crazy; it was like I had just won a million dollars, but of course I had actually received a gift that was priceless. This was a real game changer for me, and I had no idea what would happen from there on out.

23

The "The Oh God" of Vietnam

I had prayed to God, asked him to forgive me of my sins, and told him that I believed Jesus Christ had died and risen on the third day for me. Once I realized the gravity of what had taken place, I do not know how many times I said, "Oh, God, thank you." *Oh, God* is used in all kinds of expressions, but when I used it after my salvation, it took on a whole new meaning to me. When I was in Vietnam, I heard the expression *Oh, God* a lot, but most of the time it was used as an expression, not for talking to God. Some people used *Oh, God* as a means of addressing God, meaning they knew who he was, their heavenly Father. That is the only time it was used that it meant something, when it reflected a true relationship with God. Once I knew that there was truly a God and that I had prayed to Him for salvation, I started to think about the times I had heard *Oh, God,* which I believe is the most-used expression in Vietnam or any war. These are the times I remember hearing "Oh, God":

- When a soldier got wounded
- When a soldier saw another soldier get wounded
- When a sniper's bullet went flying past a soldier's head
- When someone yelled for a medic
- When we crossed a river, checked for leeches, and found at least a dozen

- When we had spent a week in the field with intense firefights and the company commander told us that we would be staying in the field for another week
- When a soldier's M-16 jammed during a firefight
- When we were on a night mission and someone tripped a wire that we knew was a booby trap
- When one of our soldier friends with whom we had just been talking seconds before lay dead on the ground
- When we saw a Vietnamese mother crying over her dead baby who had just been shot by a stray bullet
- When a soldier was sitting all alone, shaking after an intense firefight
- When a soldier got a letter from his wife or girlfriend telling him she couldn't wait for him any longer
- When we were sleeping at the base camp and, at two in the morning, we heard the siren go off and mortar rounds start coming in, prompting us to get up quickly and run to the bunker
- When a soldier was on his first mission after arriving in Vietnam and was just about to take his first step
- When a soldier got news that his grandmother had died and he knew he would miss the funeral and never see her again
- When a soldier's best friends had told him before he left for Vietnam, "Be careful and don't get yourself killed over there" and then he received a letter telling him his friend had been killed in a car crash
- When soldiers got so homesick that they actually got physically sick
- When a soldier from our barracks killed himself because he couldn't take it anymore
- When a soldier watches another shoot himself in the foot so he can get out of the field
- When a soldier was sitting in a hospital bed and realizing how close he came to dying
- When a doctor told a soldier that he would have another surgery coming up

- When a soldier started crying so hard that he couldn't talk because he was so scared
- When a soldier looked at the calendar and saw that he still had six more months to go even though it already seemed like he had been there for two years
- When a soldier walked up the ramp of the plane taking him home

You see, I heard "Oh, God" a lot and I said "Oh, God" a lot. I know that I have not listed all the times it was used. Now, I use "Oh, God" in a much different way. It is an expression of crying out to my Father and knowing that he hears me. I know that my time in Vietnam would have been different if I had already had a personal relationship with God like I do now, but I am so glad that he gave the chance to receive him as my personal savior. Oh, God, thank you for salvation and for never leaving me nor forsaking me. Amen! Oh, God, thank you for hearing my grandmother's prayers for my safety. Oh, God, thank you for allowing me to come home and now serve you. I am truly blessed.

My Call into Another Army Life

The Sunday after I received Jesus Christ as my savior, I went to church for the first time other than for a funeral or wedding. I was twenty-eight years old, and this was the first time I had been in church as a born-again Christian. Pastor John started to preach, and I was sure he was preaching directly to me because he kept looking right at me. I realize that about four thousand people were there, but his words were directed to me. I thought Sandy might have called him and told him about how I was living; it's the only way he could have known. I left that Sunday thinking about what he had said and found out later that it hadn't been him saying it; it was the Lord speaking through him. I could disagree with Pastor John, but it is hard to disagree with the Lord. Sandy asked me if I wanted to go to the Sunday night service, and I said, "We just went to church this morning. Isn't that enough?" So off we went to the Sunday night service. The crowd was a lot smaller, but it was more comfortable for me. Later that week, Sandy asked if I wanted to go to the Wednesday night service. I said, "Are you crazy? That would be three times in a week!" I said no. A few weeks later, we started to go to the Wednesday night services. Man, I had become a fanatic about this church thing, but I realized that this is a great way to grow closer to the Lord, which I started to do.

We stayed in Cincinnati for about a year and a half and decided to move back to Canton because the job was not working out like I thought it would. I called Ernie, my neighborhood friend, to see about a job at the company of which he was part owner, and he said he had a position opening up that he would give to me. I would be going into real-estate companies and trying to get them to advertise in a homes magazine. This was the second time the Lord used Ernie in my life: the first had been getting me into the Bell and Howell Corporation, which I found out later was training for my future calling.

We got settled in Canton and started looking for a church, which was not an easy thing to do. We tried many churches, but nothing was clicking in our hearts. They were all good churches, but I was looking for a sign or something. One Sunday, we went to a church to see if it was the one, and as I was walking down the aisle to find a seat, I saw one of my old neighborhood buddies sitting in a pew. Roger had been quite the character growing up in our neighborhood. He was always in a fight or getting into trouble. I yelled at him, "Roger! What are you doing here?" He looked up and yelled right back at me, "Tom! What are you doing here?" And there was my sign from the Lord—this is the church I would go to. We started hanging together along with our families. Who would have thought it— two guys from the same neighborhood becoming Christians, along with Ernie? I would have never thought that I would be doing Roger's funeral a few years after this reunion.

I don't know exactly what Sunday it was, but about six months after we had started attending Central Baptist, I walked to the front of the church during the invitation and got down on my knees at the altar. It was about two years before this that I had been on my knees in my living room having a talk with the Lord, but this time it was more of him talking to me. The Lord spoke to my heart and said that a change would be coming to me. I had no clue what that meant, but I do know I heard him tell me this as he spoke to my heart. I called Pastor Dykes, and he told me to come to his office. It felt the same as two years earlier when I had called Pastor John and he had told me to come to his office. I told Pastor Dykes what had happened to me that Sunday and, without hesitation, he said, "Maybe the Lord is calling you into the ministry full time." I had heard this before in Cincinnati, when I went up to Pastor John after a service and told him I wanted to do something for God and not just sit in the pew. The first thing that came out of his mouth was, "Maybe the Lord is calling you into full-time service." My reaction then was the same as it was at this time: I laughed and said, "There is no way the Lord is calling me into full-time service." For one thing—well, really, for many things—I had a great job making great money and things were going very well. The other thing was that I couldn't get up in front of a church and speak on the Bible. Besides that, I really did not *want* to. One other major reason I could not do this is that I stutter and have a hard time pronouncing some of the words and names in the Bible. I would make a mess of things. I figured that by this time Pastor Dykes and the Lord would understand that I was not being called into the ministry, so the feeling I had must mean something else. Of course, Pastor Dykes had to mess everything up by saying those three words: "Pray about it!" I thought, *My three reasons are enough, so what is there to pray about?* But of course, there was no way I could say no to praying to the Lord.

I started to pray, but I wasn't sincere in my prayers because I knew there was no way that he was calling this stuttering man to full-time service to Him. This went on for about a year. I tried everything to get it out of my mind because it didn't make any sense that the Lord would be calling me to that, but I couldn't get rid of it. I tried one last thing with the Lord that I know does not make any sense: I said to the Lord, "Maybe you have the wrong Tom Williams." I do know that I was talking to the all-knowing, perfect God who does not make any mistakes, but I was desperate. I went for a walk and—I remember this very well—I lifted my hands up in the air and said to the Lord, "All right, I give up. I surrender to you, and I quit fighting. I am waving my white towel of surrender. What do you want me to do?" You probably already know this, but God has never lost a fight and never will, so what was I thinking? I had just wasted a year trying to win a fight against the Lord. God is the undefeated, undisputed champion of all time. So let me give you a little piece of advice: don't try to fight with the Lord. You do not have a chance of winning. I must admit that I felt relieved after I surrendered because I hadn't been able to get peace about the subject. It would not leave me.

My next step in this new journey was going to be talking with Sandy about my decision. I really did not know what my next move was going to be after surrendering to the Lord. I sat Sandy down and told her, "I need to talk to you." I began to tell her what had just happened on the street. I said, "I don't know what I am going to do next, but I do know that I am called into full-time ministry serving the Lord." Sandy told me that she was behind me and would support me in whatever took place as a result of this. When I finally surrendered to the Lord, I had felt relieved, and I felt relieved again after Sandy said this to me. What a wife I have, what woman she is, and what a best friend she is to me.

I called this chapter "My Call into Another Army Life" because I was about to enter God's army, and now I had to go to boot camp. I had voluntarily served in the US army for two years of my life, and now I was volunteering for God's army for life. I didn't realize it at the time, but the Lord had already been training me for the ministry. When I took that job at Bell and Howell and had to speak in front of students and teachers, that was very hard training that lasted one and a half years. My training in the army taught me discipline in many areas of my life, not just the physical but also mental aspects. My year in Vietnam was also training for the ministry. All the things I saw and felt made me stronger and more compassionate toward people. It also made me appreciate life more and recognize how blessed I really am. So you see, life is a training ground that our Lord uses to make us better servants for him. I was going back into the army, but this time my company commander was Jesus Christ, and he does not make any mistakes because He is perfect.

> Thou therefore endure hardness, as a good soldier of Jesus Christ. (2 Timothy 2:3)

I now want to be the very best soldier for Jesus Christ! My injury in Vietnam came with side effects—stuttering and having a hard time pronouncing words—and there I was, about to enter a position in which I would be talking all the time. The Lord reminded me of what I had done the previous year and a half, when I talked all the time to students and parents. It was hard to argue about that, so my new journey was set to begin. The Lord also told me that he didn't care about my stuttering or having a hard time pronouncing words because He was calling my heart into full-time ministry. That was a settling factor for me, and the Lord does not make mistakes. So I prepared to go back into army life, but this army is a whole lot different than my last.

Going to Bible College

It was official: I was going into full-time ministry for the Lord because I finally said yes after a yearlong battle with the Lord. One of the main excuses, not reasons, that I gave the Lord was my speech, of which I was very self-conscious. I believe that is why I liked working for the gas company: I didn't talk to many people because I just walked around the neighborhoods by myself, reading gas meters, and getting paid well doing it. I had just left a job in which I talked in front of hundreds of people, but this would be different. I would be presenting God's Word, counseling people during difficult times in their lives, and doing funerals and weddings, and knowing all this I still said yes. The Lord spoke to me regarding my speech concern by using Moses, who tried to get out of being used by God on account of his speech problems. I am not comparing myself to Moses; I am sharing this because it encouraged me to go on and not let my speech be an obstacle. This is the passage the Lord gave me:

> And Moses said unto the Lord, O my Lord, I am not eloquent, neither heretofore, nor since thou hast spoken unto thy servant: but I am slow of speech, and of a slow tongue. And the Lord said unto him, Who hath made man's mouth? Or who maketh the dumb, or deaf, or the seeing, or the blind? Have not I the Lord? Now therefore go, and I will be with thy mouth, and teach thee what thou shalt say. (Exodus 4:10–12)

After hearing these words from the Lord, which penetrated my heart, I could only say yes. Whether it is being called into ministry full time or teaching a three-year-old class, make sure you are not giving the Lord a bunch of excuses. The Lord needs workers in all areas, so get to work.

I was shocked but grateful that the Lord had called me into full-time ministry. The enemy has never stopped reminding me of my speech situation, and it would get to me at times but never stopped me. So if you are teaching any class for the Lord, if you are a helper in a class, if you are working in the nursery, if you are a janitor, if you are mowing the grass, if you are a prayer warrior, or if you are sending cards to the church members—whatever you are doing for the Lord, don't stop, because you are working for the Lord. That is an honor, and it is not done in vain.

Okay, now what do I do? I thought. At this time, I did not know much about the Bible. Someone told me that I should go to Bible college, but just hearing the word *college* put me into cardiac arrest. I hadn't done very well in high school; I could have, but I had other things do, like football, baseball, basketball, hunting, and fishing. I was an honor student in all of those subjects. If I could go back to high school, I would do a lot better, especially now that I heard the word *college* come up. I did take wood shop in high school and did very well working with wood, which I still do today. There was a Bible college about six miles from my house to which students from all over the United States went. I signed up there to start in the fall, and I was both excited and very scared. The thought came to mind, *What about my job, where I am doing very well?* I went to the owners and told them about my plan, explaining that I would have to leave and get a job on the afternoon or midnight shift. The company was owned by five people, and all of them loved the Lord, which made it so great to work there. They had a meeting that day in which they discussed my situation, and when they came out, they asked me what time I could make it to work. I told them it would be about twelve thirty, and then they told me to come to work at that time and do as much as I could. They never decreased my salary, which was truly a blessing from the Lord.

When school started, I talked to some of the other students and found that they had moved from six states away, while I was just six miles away. Some of them worked an afternoon or midnight shift and then came to school, and there I was starting at twelve thirty and getting off at five or six. This was truly from God, and I am still grateful for what he did for me. I do not know why he did this, but I thanked Him for it all the time. I did not finish my schooling there because I was hired as the full-time janitor at the church I was attending. I know this may not make any sense, but I had total peace about it. I look back on it now and see that it was preparing me for the ministry. I did this for about a year and a half, and I kept up on my Bible training by going through correspondence courses out of Oklahoma. I started to look back on my life and see where the Lord was in many things I had gone through. I was in boot camp for the army that I was in now—God's army. Soon, I would get the call to where God wanted me to be, but I had to go through his boot camp first.

Pastor Dykes called me into his office one day and asked me if I wanted to be the next full-time youth director at the church, along with being the bus director, and of course I said yes. I did this for about five years, and those years were filled with unbelievable events that I will never forget, including the time I almost tipped over the bus filled with teens. I had it on two wheels. And Sandy and I took fifty teens on a winter retreat over the weekend, just the two of us. We rode sleds on a huge hill where it had rained over the snow, forming ice. The hall where we were staying looked like a MASH unit. I can still see the looks on the parents' faces when we all started to get off the bus. We also went canoeing and made a trip to the hospital because a girl who was allergic to bees of course got stung by a few. Another girl had a bad asthma attack. We took several mission trips to Mexico, and the parents would say, "Take care of my child." We also made an eighty-foot-by-forty-foot mud hole for the teens to do whatever they wanted to do that day. It was a blast. The greatest memory is seeing some of those teens still serving the Lord today. In fact, some are pastors, missionaries, and faithful church members.

26

Our Move to Illinois and then Back

I really thought I was going to be a seventy-year-old youth director because I truly loved being around the teens. But the Lord was calling me to be a pastor, which I did not want to do. I had a hard time with this because teaching the teens was something I loved doing, and my being like a teen made it easier. Teaching the adults was another thing; some of those adults had been Christians twice or three times as long as I had and knew their Bible. But I did not fight with the Lord about it because I had already learned that I couldn't win. I hadn't even put a résumé together yet when I received a call from a friend who told me about a church in Illinois looking for a pastor; he had given them my name. Then I got a call from the church asking if I would come preach for them on Sunday, which was Easter Sunday. After much prayer, I said that I would. We headed for Lake City, Illinois, where, by the way, there is no lake or city—just a lot of fields of corn and soybeans. The population of Lake City was 150 people. The population of the county it was in was about 13,000, which was smaller than what we were used to. We were greeted by some people of the church, and it did not take very long for me to fall in love with both the people and the church. I taught Sunday school and preached the worship service and Sunday night service. It was a wonderful weekend, and as I was driving home, I had a good feeling about being the pastor there. But I knew the Lord was in control, and I had to wait and see what he said. The church called me a week later and asked me to come back as a candidate for the pastor position there at Prairie View Baptist Church. Before we knew it, we were there, and they voted me in as their next pastor. Some of the people came to Ohio and helped us move, which was a blessing, and we got to know them better. So we were moving again out of Canton, Ohio, and it was hard because I truly thought we would not be coming back other than to visit.

Once we arrived, I started to get nervous about being a pastor. The church had just gone through a major split and were hurting, and I needed to try and help them. Well, they helped me just as much as I helped them; we were good for each other. Some of them had a strange sense of humor, which made it easy for me to fit in.

I become friends with a pastor in Decatur, Illinois, named Dave Brown. It was good for me to have someone to talk to about the ministry. I found out that his birthday was on the same date as mine and we were the same age. My dad would always joke around and tell people that I was a twin and the good one had gotten away, so I could not wait to let him know that I had found my twin and he was a Baptist pastor too. What are the odds of this happening?

Let me tell you the very first question that was asked of me as the pastor. A woman named Faye Jackson told me that she had only a few years to live because she had leukemia. She quoted these verses to me:

> Children, obey your parents in the Lord: for this is right. Honor thy father and mother; which is the first commandment with promise; That it may be well with thee, and thou mayest live long on the earth.
> (Ephesians 6:1–3)

She said, "Pastor, I have obeyed and honored my parents and still honor them, so why am I going to die so young?" At this time she was about thirty-seven years old. My thoughts went in all directions, and I thought, *This is my first question, and it could not be any more serious.* About six other people were there, and everything went silent. Everyone was looking at me for the answer to her question. I said something then that would help me for the rest of my time in my ministry: "I don't know." Some pastors do not like to say this, but I did not want to make something up just to make myself look good; this was way too serious for that type of answer. The Lord brought me to a verse about dying that says, "And it is appointed unto men once to die ..." (Hebrews 9:27). It helped me with that question. We all have an appointed time to die, and that time will be different for everyone. My time could have been at thirty-seven years old, and if it were, I would have lived long on earth because I made it to my appointed time. Age does not matter to the Lord. We are always concerned about time, but the Lord is not. When I told Faye that, she was satisfied and I was so glad. She needed to get that out of her head because the enemy would have never given her peace about it.

We had been there for about five years when the Lord began calling me back to Canton. I was not happy about it because I wanted to pastor at Prairie View until I die; going back home had not even been a thought. I had sold our home instead of renting it because I did not want any strings attaching us there. I knew that I had to obey the Lord, but this was very hard on me because I loved being at Prairie View. The same people who had helped move us there helped us move back. I was not only going back to Canton to pastor a church; I was going to start a new church in my hometown. I was forty-two years old and had no idea how to start a church, but I was going anyway. I had written my doctoral thesis on faith, and that faith was helping me right then. I really did not understand what the Lord was doing, but all I could do was obey him and watch what was going to happen.

Many pastors leave their churches on bad terms, but I was not one of them in this case. I loved the people at Prairie View, and I had truly thought we would be there until I could not pastor anymore. The move was hard for the people at Prairie View, and it was hard for my family and me. I still stay in touch with many of the people there and do cherish their friendship. My kids had good friends there, and it was hard for them to say goodbye as well. The Lord has plans for us, and sometimes we don't understand them but must trust him in all things.

27

The Start of Liberty Baptist Church

While I was still in Illinois, a friend called me and told me about an old church building that had just sold about a month earlier, and it happened to be about a mile from the high school I had attended. My friend got me the name and phone number of the man who had bought the building, and I called him that day. Bob planned to turn the old church into a daycare. I told him that I would be coming back to Canton to start a church and would be interested in renting the building. He asked me a very important question that I was afraid he would ask: "Tom, how many do you have coming to your new church?" *Okay,* I thought, *this is going to be the deal breaker.* I had a grand total of nine, which included my family and another family. When I told him that, there was a long pause, which I did not think was a good thing. I figured it meant that he was trying to catch his breath from laughing and was thinking of a gentle way to tell me no. After a few minutes, which seemed like a few hours, he said that he was a Christian man and he would rent the building to me. I must admit that I went into a mental place where I was just staring into space, not knowing how to respond I started to think that I was actually going to start a church with pews, song books, classrooms, and a pulpit. This was the first sign from the Lord that I was totally in His will; things like this rarely happen, starting a new church in an actual church. I finally answered him, and I was trying to be calm about it because I didn't want him to think he was renting to a crazy man. "Thank you so much" was my response, and I couldn't come up with any more words. Then he asked me a question that I could not believe: "Do you have a place to live?" I had not thought about it much, so I told him no, but I was going to look for a place in a few days. He told me that he had also bought the house next to the church and he would rent that to me as well. *Okay, now,* I thought, *this cannot be happening right now.* But of course I told him yes, I would love to rent the house. It went silent again because he was figuring how much rent he would charge. He said, "I will rent the church for one thousand a month and the house for five hundred a month." Once again, I went into that mental place of disbelief. *This cannot be happening!* Think about this—a man whom I had never met and was not even talking with face to face had just bought this building and house, and he got a call from a man living in Illinois asking him to rent the church. And he offered the house as well for fifteen hundred dollars, and the deal was made. I was thinking, *How did this just happen?* and he must have thought, *What did I just do?* Talk about the Lord being in all of this. It truly came from him, and once again, I thanked Him over and over.

Once I hung up the phone I started to scream and scream and then scream some more. I really could not believe what had just happened. I settled down, calming my emotions, and a major thought came to mind: *He said fifteen hundred dollars.* I didn't have a job, and I had a grand total of nine people who would be coming to church. *How in the world am I going to come up with fifteen hundred dollars a month, not just for the first month but for the months ahead?* I jumped back into my flesh and said, "What have I just done? There is no way that this can be done." I thought of the utilities that must be paid also, and don't forget about the insurance for the places. I hoped the other family who was coming was worth millions. I knew that wasn't the case, but it was a good thought. Once I went through all those thoughts, I finally came to rest on this: *I know this is God's will, so he will work all that stuff out.* I called my old friend Ernie and told him, "I am coming back to Canton to start a church. Do you have any job openings?" Once again, he came through, this time with a part-time job for me, and he threw in a bonus: he hired Sandy also, but she was full time. Listen, when things like this happen, all I can say is "Thank you Lord for your love and care."

Then came one of those hard things that I hate to do, and that is moving away from people whom we truly love. That is what we felt for the people of Prairie View Baptist Church. We really loved them, and they had been so kind and generous to us. I felt guilty and very sad as we pulled away for the last time as their pastor and friends. I knew it was the Lord's will, but it still was a very hard thing to do. We arrived in Canton in the first week of July 1992 and moved into our home next to the church. I still did not know what to do about starting a church, so I called the Christian Law Association, and they walked me through everything and did it for free. They called places for me and got the paperwork ready, and all I did was sign them. I cannot thank them enough. I would still be trying to figure things out if it weren't for them.

I did not have to make our first payment until August 1, which gave me some time to save up the rent money. I did not want to discourage Bob by not paying the rent or paying just part of it. During the month of July, we passed out flyers throughout the neighborhood and received free advertisements on the radio and in the local newspaper. As we were passing out the flyers, we came to the house of Gary and Diana Mencer and found out they were looking for a new church home. We talked, and they said they would come. *Hey, that's twelve!* I thought. They had a son, and we were a growing church without even having our first service. I had led Gary to the Lord years before this; again, thank you, Lord, because this was very encouraging to us, and they are still members today. Raoul and Chris Vitale saw the article about the church starting on Perry Road that had a picture of Sandy and me standing in front of the church building. They were looking for a church and figured they would go to ours and see what it was all about. I think they liked it because they are still going to Liberty these thirty years later.

The day came when the doors of Liberty Baptist Church would open for the first time. It was so exciting that I could hardly stand up, and it was so scary that I could hardly stand up. It was August 2, 1992, a beautiful day. The sun was shining, and I don't believe there was a cloud in the sky, which is very unusual in Ohio. The church building had been built in 1919 and had a church bell on the top. I didn't know when it had last been rung, but I rang it that morning and it sounded so beautiful. I couldn't believe it when the people started to come; many of my friends and relatives came to support me for this first service. I preached the first service at Liberty Baptist Church, but I don't remember too much about that day. My mind was going everywhere. When the service was over and everyone went home, I was exhausted, not just from the day but from leaving Prairie View, moving back to Canton, walking all over the place passing out flyers, working at my new job, getting my message together, and of course thinking about the offering. Now, I know that might not sound good, but I am not going to lie: it was going through my mind. We counted the money, and take a guess what it came to. You're right—fifteen hundred dollars. I could not believe it, but I should have known. Our God is a good God. We never missed one payment to Bob, and we both knew that the Lord was all over this.

Let me say something here that I believe needs to be said. I did not start Liberty, nor am I its founder. The Lord knew all about Liberty, and he wanted me to be its first pastor. The Lord is the founder of Liberty Baptist Church, not me. I thank Him for allowing me to be the first pastor. In the church world, people are not supposed to go back to their hometowns to pastor. I know without a doubt this is God's will because he has put his stamp of approval on so many things. One of them was when another pastor called me up and asked me out for breakfast. We met, and he told me that he and about six other pastors would get together once a week and pray that a good church would start in that building, and they were so thankful that Liberty was there. Another church gave us a piano, which was a blessing; another church gave us some kids chairs for the classes; and another church gave us monthly support for the first year. These are all stamps of approval from the Lord, and there were many more, which I already wrote about.

About six months later, my mom came to visit me in my office at the church. We talked about all the things that were going well for Liberty and about our family. When I had first received Jesus Christ as my Savior, I talked to my mom about her salvation. She told me she was all right and wouldn't talk to me any more about it. In my office that day, I brought up again where she would go when she dies, and she told me she was not sure. I had the awesome privilege of showing my mother through the Bible how to receive Jesus Christ as her Savior. She prayed with me that day, and I will see her in heaven someday. Amen and amen! That is what I called a big stamp of approval on my move back to Canton.

28

Living Life Can Make You or Break You

When my grown kids would call me and start to complain about something, which we all do at times, I would tell them the same thing: "Do you know what this is called? Life—it's called life." Life teaches us every day. We can learn from it and become better people, or we can keep on complaining about it and become bitter and angry. The choice is ours to make and nobody else's. I think about getting shot in the mouth as an eighteen-year-old kid, a teenager fighting in a war with real guns, with real people trying to kill me. How could that change a person for the better? It can, and it did for me. How could all the things that went on while I was in Vietnam change me for the better? They have because I chose to be better because of them. The alternative was to become bitter and angry for the rest of my life, and I did not want to do that. Life will bring you things that can crush and destroy you. I know because I have lived a long time and have seen many crushing things take place in my life and others. I held the hand of a dear, faithful Christian friend who was forty-two while she took her last breath, and then I went out of the room to tell her husband that she had passed away. I have seen diseases destroy people physically and mentally. I have done a funeral for a one-month-old baby and tried to help the parents. I have had parents in my office crying as they told me about their son's committing suicide. Sandy and I went to the hospital and saw our daughter's head caved in from a rock that a robber smashed into her. I could go on and on, and I know you could add to this, but how do we get through it without letting it damaging us? If you are not a Christian, I do not know how you get through it, but I do know how Christians get through it. We must become doers of God's Word and not just hearers of his Word; this is the most important thing that Christians receive into their hearts. "But be ye doers of the word, and not hearers only, deceiving your own selves" (James 1:22). As Christians, our true help comes from God, from becoming doers of His Word. Too many Christians hear from God but do not apply His Word, especially when life gets hard. "Peace I leave with you, my peace I give unto you: not as the world giveth, give I unto you. Let not your heart be troubled, neither let it be afraid" (John 14:27). The Lord is telling you not to be troubled or afraid even in the hard times of life. This may sound hard to do, and you are right, but with the Lord on your side you can do it. We take on many cares as we go through life, some more than others, but I do know the one who will take those cares from you. "Casting all your care upon him: for he careth for you" (1 Peter 5:7). And there is also this verse from the Lord: "Come unto me, all ye that labour and heavy laden, and I will give you rest" (Matthew 11:28). Listen, the Lord did not put these words in the Bible so we would have good things to read. The Lord wants us to be doers of His Word because He knows that it will help us get through the hard times. I am not trying to preach here; I am just trying to help anyone who is reading this book and going through hard times. They might be related to Vietnam or something else, but we all have hard times. We must trust in the Lord at all times, not just when things are going well for us. "Trust in the Lord with all thine heart; and lean not unto thine own understanding" (Proverbs 3:5). If we can trust a pilot to fly us thirty thousand feet in the air in a steel container, then we can surely trust in the Almighty God.

Trusting in the Lord and applying His Word in our lives is the difference in having peace in any situation, even if we don't understand it or become more and more bitter or angry with each situation that comes arises. As I am writing this book at the age of seventy-two and looking back on my life, I can see that there have been some very difficult times, and if I had not trusted in the Lord and done what He said, then I would be a different person and would not be writing this book. I hope this chapter has been a blessing and a help because it is all about Jesus and nothing about me.

You may be thinking, *It can't be that easy, but it truly is*. You may still have to go through things you do not like, but if you give them to the Lord, then you will go through them with peace in your heart. You may still be wondering, *How do I give it to the Lord?* and that is a great question. Find a place where you can be alone and start talking to the Lord. Say, "Lord, I am giving this to you, and please give me your peace so that, as a child of God, I will be able to show others how God works in his children during tough times. Amen." The Lord loves his children and wants to help them and comfort them in everything they go through; this is something you must believe. Don't let the situations of life beat you down so that you stay down. You can get back up with the help of the Lord, so allow Him to be part of everything you go through.

29

Back to Liberty Baptist Church

The previous chapter talked about life, and life is a school that we all are going through. We are taught everyday about something on every subject imaginable. During the first year of Liberty Baptist Church, we had many ups and downs, but mostly ups. After a year went by, we bought the house next to the church, then we bought the church building, and then we bought the house behind the church with an extra lot, which became an additional parking lot. I must admit that, at this point, I was a little overwhelmed by what the Lord had done for Liberty in its first two years. A lot of praying and fasting went on to get to this place. As time progressed, we started to grow and space was limited, so we started to think about a new building, which made me shake when I thought about it too much. I started to look for some land, which was really hard to find, but I kept looking and praying, knowing that the Lord had some land out there for us. Soon, we found ten acres of land about three miles from our church. I never dreamed that we would get land, let alone ten acres, but the Lord gave it to us. The price was incredible, and it was in a great spot to build a church. We bought the land for ninety thousand dollars, and all we could say was, "Thank you, Lord."

We bought this land in our eighth year of Liberty, thinking we would start building in a few years. About seven years went by, and we were not close to being able to build our new church. We had to do something, so we thought about selling the land because we didn't have enough money to start building a garage, let alone a building. We were about a week away from putting the land up for sale and possibly merging with another church. I was teaching at Massillon Baptist College when one of the students raised his hand and gave a testimony about a foundation helping his church build a new church. As he was speaking, my heart was pounding, so I went to him after class, got his pastor's phone number, and called him as soon as I could. From him I got the address of the foundation and sent them the information about what we were doing. They sent an application, and it took me a while to answer all the questions; they wanted to determine who we were and what we wanted to do. About four or five hundred churches would send them applications each year for help. They would help about two or three a year, so I knew that the Lord would have to be involved if we were to be one of them.

I would go to pastors conferences, and there would always be a pastor who would stand up and give a testimony about how they had received a lot of money for a building or some other project. I was thinking what most of the other pastors were thinking: *It would be nice for that to happen to us. Hey, if the Lord gave them money to build, why wouldn't he do that for us?* About two months later, and I received a letter from the foundation, and I shook while opening it. The letter said that they were sorry, but they could not help us and explained that it was very hard for them to choose whom they would help. They prayed over all the applications before they decided who, they would help. I was very disappointed, but I totally understood. And I knew that the Lord was involved whether we got the money or not. About three weeks went by, and we were preparing to sell the land once again. I received another letter from the foundation, and this time I opened it up right away, thinking it was a follow-up letter for the last one. The letter said that they were, in fact, going to help us, and it included a check for $150,000. It said they would send another $150,000 when we needed it. I did the math, and that comes up to $300,000. (I am good at math.) My emotions calmed right away. Because of that first letter I had received from them, I thought the deacons were playing a really bad joke on me. I took the check to the bank and explained, "This check is probably not real, but let's see what happens." I didn't tell anyone about it except for Sandy, and we kept it a secret to see if the check would go through. I didn't want to give the deacons a hint of me receiving the letter because I wanted this cruel joke to backfire on them. The bank called me about five days later and said the check had gone through. The person on the phone added, "You have $150,000 in your account." No one has any idea what I was feeling. Even I don't know, but I knew what the person at the bank had just told me: Liberty Baptist Church had $150,000 in our account, and we would get another $150,000 when we needed it. Did I tell you what the total was? Three hundred thousand dollars!

Let me go back about eight years before we received the money. I got a call about a man who had been falsely accused of murdering his mother-in-law and raping his niece. The caller wanted to know if I would go visit him in jail, which was about a half hour away. I know that what I am about to say sounds really bad, but I was very busy at this time with a lot of things going on, and I thought I would go see him, have a word of prayer with him, put him on my prayer list, and go on with my life. I went to visit Clarence and spent about two hours with him, and I could already tell that he hadn't done what he was accused of by what he was saying to me. I did pray with him, and I told him my initial plans about this visit. I asked the Lord to forgive me, and I asked him to forgive me. I told Clarence that I would not leave him and would be his pastor and friend from then on—and I meant it. I told him I would help him in every way I could to get him out of this.

He had been identified as a suspect when the niece said the assailant might have looked like Uncle Clarence, but she was six years old and had just been brutally raped. I told Clarence and the family that the only way he would be found guilty was if it was the Lord's will. Clarence was found guilty and sentenced to fifty-five years in prison, and everyone was in total shock. As Clarence was led out of the courtroom, he said it was going to be okay. The words I had said about this being the Lord's will came back to me. I spent the next seven and a half years raising money for detective work and blood work. I visited Clarence in prison many times, and we would always talk about the Lord and at times have Bible studies. The man who had actually committed this horrible crime was moved to Clarence's cell block, and Clarence was able to retrieve a cigarette butt this man had used and send it to his lawyers. It was a miracle that it made it through because all letters were inspected before leaving the prison. This man's sample matched all the blood in the house where this crime had occurred, and oh yeah, this man lived next door. Clarence was set free after spending seven and a half years in prison for something he did not do. I still remember seeing his face when he walked out of that prison as a free man; I will never forget it. A few months later he received a settlement for being falsely imprisoned, and he wanted to tithe it to the church. That money paid for the architect who was designing our new church building. I am not saying that is the reason Clarence went to prison, but I am saying this: the Lord took something bad and made something good come from it. "And we know that all things work together for good to them that love God, to them who are called according to his purpose" (Romans 8:28). Clarence gave the church more money later, which also went towards our new building.

About six months before we were to start building, I saw another church being built and stopped to talk to the foreman of the project, and he gave me a business card. I called Berlin Construction and talked to Gid, a Christian man, and his estimate was a lot lower than the others we had gotten. His company liked to help churches as much as they could, and they truly did that for us. I was able to get our own plumber, drywall installer, lights, and carpet, and Berlin Construction allowed us to do some of the work on the church, which saved us thousands of dollars. We built a twelve-thousand-square-foot building on ten acres of land, and I have still not gotten over it yet or stopped thanking the Lord because it was all him. The Lord truly does work in ways we will never understand, but we don't have to; we just need to trust Him in all things. "Trust in the Lord with all thine heart; and lean not unto thine own understanding" (Proverbs 3:5).

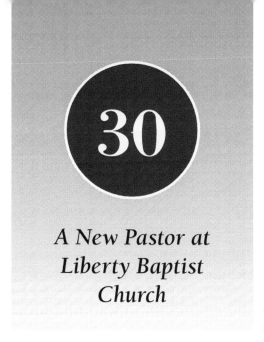

30

A New Pastor at Liberty Baptist Church

The church was doing well, and I knew that the time was coming when I would need to step down as its pastor. So I started trying to figure out how this was going to happen. Right down the street from the church, I had seen a man working on a rundown house almost every day, so I stopped in one day to see all the remodeling that he was doing. He said his name was Luke Vaughn and that he was married with three children. I had no idea that the Lord had just introduced me to the next pastor of Liberty Baptist Church. After I went to his house to see how he was doing many times, he finished, and his family moved into their newly remodeled home. They started to come to Liberty and began serving the Lord right away. The people of Liberty fell in love with them quickly because they were so excited to be there and to serve the Lord. Luke and Jen reminded Sandy and me of ourselves when we were that age.

About five years after they had first come Liberty, Luke came into my office and told me that the Lord was calling him into full-time ministry. This was about the time I was starting to think about stepping down in about four or five years. I told Luke that he must have total peace on being called into the ministry because he would be forsaking everything and totally following the Lord; I said that Jen must have peace about it also. Even at this point, I was not thinking about Luke being Liberty's next pastor; the thought did not cross my mind.

It seemed like just yesterday when we had held our first service at Liberty, and now we were in our new building on ten acres of land. It was like having a baby, watching it grow up, and then having to let it go. That is how I thought about this, but I knew and had total peace that stepping down was the right thing to do. I wanted to find a young man with a young family to take my place. A few years after Luke's calling and his not having peace about going to the churches that wanted him, we ordained him as an associate pastor of Liberty. At this time, I had peace about talking to Luke about being the next pastor. We both fasted and prayed about it, and both of us had total peace. However, it was a difficult decision for both of us. I would be stepping down from being the pastor of Liberty after almost thirty years, and Luke was going to be the next pastor. I don't mean to sound like I am someone special because I am not. What I mean is that, since I had been at Liberty for all those years, things had gone a certain way for a long time, and I knew Luke would have different ways of doing things, which is only right. But people do not like change unless they bring it on themselves.

As the days got closer to my stepping down, I went through many emotions, and the next big thing came in front of Sandy and me. We would have to leave the church to give Luke full rein without my being in the way, not that I would try to be in the way. I did not want the people coming to Sandy or me because I wanted Luke to be the pastor. Luke and I had another meeting, and this time Luke asked me to stay at Liberty and teach the adult Sunday school class. I really did not know what to say, so I told Luke I would have to pray about it. After prayer and fasting, I received total peace on staying. I sought counsel from many people, and all but one told me I must leave Liberty, so this was a very hard decision to make. But the Lord gave me an answer that both Sandy and I really wanted to hear.

On Sunday, March 7, 2021, I announced that I would be stepping down as the pastor of Liberty Baptist Church and that Luke would become the next pastor provided he got voted in, and he did. I was a wreck after making this announcement, but I also was relieved. It was over and it was official; I would no longer be the pastor of Liberty Baptist Church.

It didn't seem to be that long ago when I was graduating from high school and or when I was jumping off that carrier in Vietnam to go on my first combat mission as an eighteen-year-old kid. Time sure does go flying by, and it hasn't slowed up yet.

It has been a year since I stepped down, and the church is going well, with new members and new things happening. Pastor Luke has done a great job in his first year, and I have done a great job staying out of his way. Jen, Luke's wife, has also done a great job as the pastor's wife; she is truly a servant of the Lord. I don't know what the Lord has planned for Liberty, but I am glad I am a part of it along with Sandy.

31

My Heroes of the Faith

A hero is a person who is admired or idealized for courage, outstanding achievements, or noble qualities. As I look back on my forty years in the ministry, I can identify six heroes who have helped me throughout my time in serving the Lord.

- Jesus Christ is my hero, but He is much more than that. Jesus is my savior, my Lord, my fortress, my protector, and I could go on and on. I am going to heaven and will live there forever, without any more pain, suffering, tears, or death, all because of Jesus Christ.

- Jim Delaschmit was an evangelist whom I first heard speak as a young Christian in a Kentucky church. Jim had been saved out of being the president of the Hell's Angels in Missouri. He had an incredible testimony about his life and was a well-known evangelist and great singer. I was able to get Jim to preach a youth revival at the church I was serving. We formed a great relationship from that time until the time he went home to be with the Lord. Jim helped me with many things I went through as I served the Lord. He was my encourager, which I needed at times.

- Garvin Dykes was the pastor of the church we settled into after we moved back to Canton. I was called into the ministry under his leadership and then became the youth director there. I don't know how many times I knocked on Pastor Dykes's door to ask him questions, but it was a lot. When I was a new pastor at my first church in Illinois, I called Pastor Dykes on a regular basis and asked him some questions that he had never heard before. One time he asked me, "Brother Williams, what have you gotten yourself into over there?" The church had gone through a bad split, and I ran into many situations in which I didn't know what to do. The Lord put Pastor Dykes in my life to help me in many things, and he was truly a blessing to me. I want to call him up right now and ask him what heaven is like.

- Carlos Demarest was a missionary to Mexico. Sandy and I took the youth on about four mission trips to Mexico, and that is where we met Carlos. There were times when I got so mad at him, and there were times when I would cry when I heard of his burden for the Mexican people. Carlos thought that if people were not called to be missionaries to Mexico, they were not right with the Lord. He would take us places where we had to build bridges to get the bus across a river or low area. Carlos would tell us that no white man had ever been to this village; what a blessing it was to go into that village knowing that. Carlos is in heaven today enjoying the fruits of his labor, and yes, he is in the Mexican section.

- Terry "Shrek" Nalian was an evangelist from Michigan. One of my students at Massillon Baptist College called me and told me about this evangelist that I must have at my church. The name of the ministry was the Stand Strength Team, and they would go into schools and break bats, bend bars, and rip phone books in half. Then they would invite the kids to the church that was sponsoring them at night. When I first talked to Shrek on the phone, I fell in love with this man because I heard his burden for the kids and teens of the world. In fact, I asked the church to take his group on for support as our missionaries, and we did without even seeing them in person. They later came to our church, and Shrek and I formed a relationship or bond right from the start. We clicked from the beginning, and it never ended until he went to be with the Lord. Shrek and I would go back and forth discussing the Bible, sometimes for hours. He had most of the Bible memorized; I had never met anyone like him. I called him a walking concordance. We would call to encourage each other, and we always did. We were passionate about our sports, too. He was a Michigan man and I am an Ohio man, so we were always going back and forth. I would send him things about the Indians, Browns, and Ohio State all the time. When his group was with us for a meeting, I put Browns stickers on their car and van bumpers. I didn't realize it at the time, but our relationship was good for both of us because it allowed us to get away from the ministry. We needed that because we both put everything we had into our service for the Lord.

- All my heroes of the faith are in heaven now except for one, which seems impossible. I saved my best hero for last: Sandy Williams, my wife, my partner, and my very best friend. As I am writing this, we have been married for fifty-three years. We started to date when we were juniors in high school, and we were even in the second grade together and didn't know it until later. There is no doubt that I would not be where I am today without Sandy. She is the very best Christian woman that I know and have ever known. She is my rock, and I would be sinking without her in my life. She is the best mother I have ever seen and a blessing to more than I could mention. Sandy has stuck by me through situations in which many women would have left their husbands. She has trusted me in so many decisions that I have made that I can't believe it. If any women reading this want to know how to be the best wife, friend, and Christian woman, get a hold of Sandy Williams because she is all the above.

32

A Story of Riches

Everybody has a story to tell, and this has been mine. It is divided into two completely different stories or lives. The first twenty-eight years of my life I refer to as BC, "before Christ." I was making all of my decisions based on myself and how I felt about things. When I did talk to God during those first twenty-eight years, it was like talking to a stranger because I didn't have a relationship with him yet. From the twenty-ninth year on is AC, "after Christ." I have heard some, including myself, say, "I am waiting for my ship to come in so I can be rich" or "I am waiting for my rich uncle to die so I will inherit a lot of money." The word *rich* means many things to many people, and I found out what it really means after I became a Christian. When I accepted Jesus Christ as my personal Savior, that made me very rich. When the Lord told me He wanted me to have an abundant life and I went on to have one, that makes me rich. Seeing my entire family accept Jesus Christ as their Savior makes me rich. Having peace in the most difficult times of life made me rich. God's calling me into full-time ministry even though I left a great job where I made a lot more money has made me rich. Knowing God will forgive and forget my sins if I am truthful when I ask him to makes me rich. Having my relationship with Sandy, my best friend, grow makes me rich. God's placing people in my life at the right times to help me get through things makes me rich. Seeing many of the teens who were in our youth group some thirty-five years ago go on to become youth directors, pastors, and missionaries, serving the Lord in local churches, makes me rich. Watching God give us the money to go on mission trips to Mexico, Canada, Peru, Ecuador, and Africa makes me rich. Seeing how the Lord has blessed Liberty Baptist Church all these years makes me rich. Watching the Lord use an eighteen-year-old kid who got shot in the mouth to lead people to the Lord and help people who are suffering makes me rich. Watching the Lord heal my daughter Julie when she was about to have a kidney transplant makes me rich. Seeing my daughter Janis heal after being brutally attack by a robber makes me rich. Knowing that, one day, I will take my last breath on this earth knowing I will take my next breath in heaven makes me rich. I could fill pages and pages discussing what has made me rich in this life because I *am* rich spiritually, and my relationship with my heavenly Father is priceless.

I will conclude my book with this: Thank you, Lord, for saving my soul and for all the riches you have given me. God is good—all the time!

Made in the USA
Monee, IL
16 March 2023

30007690R00081